W9-BYB-465

The Great STEWARDSHIP ADVENTURE FOR KIDS

PATRICIA J. MOORHEAD
&
DAVID N. JOBE

Gospel Light

HOW TO MAKE CLEAN COPIES FROM THIS BOOK

You may make copies of portions of this book with a clean conscience if
- you (or someone in your organization) are the original purchaser;
- you are using the copies you make for a noncommercial purpose (such as teaching or promoting your ministry) within your church or organization;
- you follow the instructions provided in this book.

However, it is ILLEGAL for you to make copies if
- you are using the material to promote, advertise or sell a product or service other than for ministry fund-raising;
- you are using the material in or on a product for sale; or
- you or your organization are not the original purchaser of this book.

By following these guidelines you help us keep our products affordable.
Thank you,
Gospel Light

Permission to make photocopies or to reproduce by any other mechanical or electronic means in whole or in part any designated* page, illustration or activity in this book is granted only to the original purchaser and is intended for noncommercial use within a church or other Christian organization. None of the material in this book may be reproduced for any commercial promotion, advertising or sale of a product or service. Sharing of the material in this book with other churches or organizations not owned or controlled by the original purchaser is also prohibited. All rights reserved.

*Pages with the following notation can be legally reproduced:
© 2000 by Gospel Light. Permission to photocopy granted. *The Great Stewardship Adventure for Kids*

Editorial Staff
Publisher, William T. Greig • **Senior Consulting Publisher,** Dr. Elmer L. Towns • **Publisher, Research, Planning and Development,** Billie Baptiste • **Managing Editor,** Lynnette Pennings, M.A. • **Senior Consulting Editors,** Dr. Gary S. Greig, Wesley Haystead, M.S.Ed.• **Senior Editor, Theological and Biblical Issues,** Bayard Taylor, M.Div. • **Editor,** Sheryl Haystead • **Editorial Team,** Mary Gross, Karen McGraw • **Contributing Editor,** Amanda Abbas • **Designer,** Carolyn Thomas • **Illustrators,** Curtis Dawson, Colleen Kennelly, Roger Mejia

Scripture quotations are taken from the *Holy Bible, New International Version*®. Copyright © 1973, 1978, 1984 by International Bible Society. Used by permission of Zondervan Publishing House. All rights reserved.

© 2000 by Gospel Light, Ventura, CA 93006. All rights reserved. Printed in the U.S.A.

CONTENTS

How to Use This Book

The purpose of this course is to help kids establish a lifelong commitment to stewardship. Understanding how they can practice good stewardship in their everyday lives is fundamental to the understanding students develop of their role in the Church. Seeing how their individual gifts and abilities contribute to the life and work of God's family nurtures in them self-esteem, a sense of identity and a heart-felt knowledge that they belong to God and His Church.

This course begins by discussing the importance of the right attitudes about stewardship and progresses to describe specific actions students can take. Included are

- **Bible stories**
- **Learning activities**—games, art projects, service projects, etc.
- **Memory verses**
- **Discussion questions**
- **Wrap-up sessions** to review the lesson and the course
- An on-going **prayer journal**
- **Take-home papers** with daily devotions, puzzles, life-application stories about stewardship, etc.

All of these resources are geared to help children become educated—and excited—about stewardship for their whole lives.

And the lessons are flexible because you choose from the learning activity options. The person who knows your needs best—you!—can choose and assemble each day's program to fit your needs and time schedule.

Plus, each lesson can be taught individually, which allows you to create your own course if you need a shorter one. Below are suggestions for four- or eight-week courses:

Four-Week Course:

Lesson 1: Heart Matters in Stewardship

Lesson 5: Treasure Trove

Lesson 10: Trusted to Share the Good News

Lesson 13: For God's Glory

Eight-Week Course:

Lesson 1: Heart Matters in Stewardship

Lesson 4: Earth and All Belong to God

Lesson 5: Treasure Trove

Lesson 9: Total Fitness

Lesson 10: Trusted to Share the Good News

Lesson 11: Together, Much Can Be Accomplished

Lesson 13: For God's Glory

So get ready to embark on *The Great Stewardship Adventure for Kids!*

© 2000 Gospel Light. Permission to photocopy granted. *The Great Stewardship Adventure for Kids*

Schedule

FOR A PERFECT FIT, CUSTOMIZE IT!

Schedule
1.
2.
3.
4.

Every group of students is different: Every class varies in age, maturity level and socioeconomic status, as well as gender groupings (all-boy, all-girl or mixed classes).

Some classes may have students steeped in Bible knowledge as well as students who have never been to church before.

Every teacher is different, too! Some prefer games, some prefer discussion, and some prefer creating art that reinforces the lesson.

Each class has a different amount of time available.

That's why this curriculum is designed to be as flexible as possible. Not every activity will work in every class, but activity choices give you the opportunity to customize the lesson for the individuals in your class. Complete lesson plans will meet students' needs for involvement as well as give you opportunities to build the relationships with your students that make the difference between simply conducting a class and leading students to follow your example in knowing and loving Jesus Christ.

GETTING PREPARED

We understand what a commitment it is to prepare a weekly lesson. We have designed this course with you, the teacher, in mind. Take time to read and consider both the Teacher's Devotional and the Scripture passages listed for every lesson, as well as to note the materials listed for the next week's lesson. Many teachers find that by beginning on Sunday night, they think about the lesson during the week and are better prepared.

GETTING STARTED

5-15 MINUTES

GETTING STARTED activities help build relationships among students and start them thinking about the topic of the day in a thought-provoking or lighthearted way.

GETTING INTO GOD'S WORD

20-30 MINUTES

The goal of every **GETTING INTO GOD'S WORD** segment is to guide students to read, study and discuss the Bible for themselves.

✓ Each student or pair of students needs a Bible. If students do not bring Bibles from home, provide classroom Bibles and bookmarks (slips of paper, student-decorated index cards, etc.).

✓ Questions are provided throughout the Bible Study to help students develop Bible study skills and to keep students thinking about the study. Be aware of the Bible skills level of each student and provide assistance accordingly, in a way that doesn't embarrass students.

✓ Tailor the Bible Study time to the needs of your own class. For example, students who are familiar with an event or character in a Bible Study may be invited to tell the story action, while you supply details from Scripture and/or the Bible Study to complete their information.

✓ The Conclusion at the end of each Bible Study gives a brief summary to help you make sure your students have a clear understanding of the lesson's Bible truth.

GETTING FOCUSED

20-30 MINUTES

You may choose between the two **GETTING FOCUSED** activities or use them both, if time allows. These activities will help your students understand the relationship between the Bible truth they have studied and their day-to-day experiences.

✓ Thought-provoking discussion questions are provided to help you guide the students to think and respond as you lead them to complete either of the activities. Again, consider the individuals in your class: students who have attended church a great deal will be able to discuss questions that new students may find incomprehensible; some students have a high need for movement; some have poorly developed verbal skills; and so on. (If you teach with another teacher, consider having both of you lead an activity. Using more than one type of activity provides balance and variety for your students.)

✓ Activities may include:

• an **Active Focus** activity—a game or game-like activity that incorporates physical movement with discussion;

• a **Service Focus** activity—a way to apply Bible truth to life by serving others;

• an **Art Focus** activity—a creative way for each student to reinforce the lesson.

✓ Use of the discussion questions will be most effective and meaningful if you maintain a ratio of one teacher for every six to eight students, with no more than 30 students in a classroom. Recruit parent-helpers to assist; they can participate in their child's class for four or five lessons at a time. Also keep in mind that energetic preteens learn best in a room with adequate space for active participation: 25 to 30 square feet for each student.

FINAL FOCUS

FINAL FOCUS time provides a natural conclusion to the **GETTING FOCUSED** segment. Every week, you will bring the class notebook (a purchased spiral-bound notebook) to help students record and remember the ideas they feel are most important in each lesson. The class notebook will also include a prayer journal section, giving your class the opportunity to journal prayer requests and answers as well as participating in a variety of prayer activities.

 © 2000 Gospel Light. Permission to photocopy granted. *The Great Stewardship Adventure for Kids*

Heart Matters in Stewardship

LIFE FOCUS

God wants us to be good stewards of His gifts for our whole lives.

① GETTING PREPARED

AIMS

DISCUSS the meaning of stewardship—to care for something that belongs to someone else;

RECOGNIZE God wants us to use His gifts wisely;

EXPLORE ways we can be stewards of God's gifts to us for our whole lives.

SCRIPTURE

Matthew 25:14-29

KEY VERSE

"Whatever you do, work at it with all your heart, as working for the Lord, not for men." Colossians 3:23

Teacher's Devotional

Christian stewardship can be defined as "faith in action." When we hear God's Word, understand it and obey what it says, we begin to live our faith, not just talk about it. So then, stewardship is the result of God making us able by His grace to live as joyful, efficient stewards of His gifts to us for the greater purpose of His kingdom.

What does it mean to be a "good steward"? A modern concept would be that of the manager of a business. He or she may make decisions, count the money and run the business, but the manager is not the owner. He or she does not have ultimate authority or keep the proceeds. The parable of the talents develops this analogy to help us understand who our master is, know what He requires and remember how we will have to account for the things with which He entrusts us.

© 2000 Gospel Light. Permission to photocopy granted. *The Great Stewardship Adventure for Kids*

Take time to study and pray about each lesson in the days before you teach. God will bless the extra effort you take in preparing each lesson—and by preparing carefully, you will be a model of good stewardship! As you and your students discover the varied aspects of stewardship, you not only may discover exciting opportunities but also may well discover a new joy in "managing God's business," serving the King!

2 GETTING STARTED

Buried Treasure

Materials: Bible, variety of colored paper, scissors, marker, large box, Styrofoam peanuts or other packing material, masking tape, large sheet of paper.

Preparation: One color at a time, cut paper into six to eight circles each approximately 2 inches (5 cm) in diameter to represent coins, and print two or three words of Colossians 3:23 on each paper coin. Create one complete set of verse coins for each group of three to four students, each set having a different color of paper. Hide paper coins in large box half full of Styrofoam peanuts or other packing material. Create a masking-tape line on one side of classroom and place box on opposite side of room. (Optional: Hide paper coins around classroom.)

Procedure: Divide group into teams of six to eight. Assign a color to each team. Teams line up behind masking-tape line to run a relay. Students search box to find a paper coin in their team's color and then return to team to put coins in memory verse order. To check their work, ask a volunteer to read Colossians 3:23 aloud. **What does this verse tell us to do? Why?** (Work with our whole heart. We are working for God.) **In the coming weeks, we will study what it means to work with all our hearts for the Lord. We will use the term "stewardship" often.** Print "stewardship" on large paper. **What does "stewardship" mean?** Volunteers respond. **"Stewardship" means using and taking care of things that belong to someone else. If someone loans you his or her CD player, how can you be a good steward of it?** (Take care of it. Not lose it.) **As members of God's family, God gives us many wonderful gifts, and we can be good stewards of those gifts. Today we'll hear about three men who had some different ideas about what stewardship means.**

3 GETTING INTO GOD'S WORD

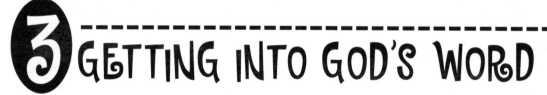

Materials: Bibles; optional—coins.

Bible Study

Students find Matthew 25:14-29 in their Bibles. As you lead the following study, help students to discover answers in their Bibles.

Has anyone ever asked you to feed his or her pet while he or she went on vacation? to water the plants or mow the lawn? What did you do? Volunteers answer. **Jesus told a story about what three people did when they were asked to take care of money for someone else.**

© 2000 Gospel Light. Permission to photocopy granted. *The Great Stewardship Adventure for Kids*

Once there was a wealthy man who was about to go on a long trip. And while the man was gone, he knew he wouldn't be able to take care of his business as usual. So he did something to make sure his money kept earning more money.

The master went to three of his servants and gave each of them a HUGE amount of his money to take care of. **Read Matthew 25:15 to find how much money he gave to the first servant.** (Optional: Count out the appropriate number of coins to represent talents.) To the first servant he said, "Here are five talents." In those days, a "talent" was a huge sum of money. To the second servant he gave two talents. And to the third servant he gave one talent. Then the master left on his trip.

Read Matthew 25:16 to find out what the first servant did after his master left. At once the servant with five talents went to work, using the money he'd been given to make more money for his master's business. In fact, during the time the master was gone, this hardworking servant earned five MORE talents—twice as much as he had started with!

The second servant also hurried to work. He carefully invested and used the master's money. And like the servant who started with the five talents, the second servant doubled his money, too! He earned TWO more talents. **How much money do you think the last servant made? Read Matthew 25:18 to find out!**

Even though it wasn't as much as the other two had been given, the amount of money the third servant had was still huge. But instead of investing the money and using it to make more money for his master, he dug a hole in the ground. He laid the money in the bottom of the hole and filled the hole with dirt!

A long time later, the master of these servants returned. He called the three together to see what they had done with his money.

The servant who had earned five more talents gave them to his master saying, "You gave me five talents and see—I have earned five more for you!"

What do you think the master said to the servant? Read Matthew 25:21. The master was glad that the first servant handled his money wisely. Now he was going to reward the servant by giving the servant even MORE to take care of and invest!

The second servant came to his master. He laid the money he had earned on the table, saying to his master, "Sir, you gave me two talents. Now I have earned two more talents for you."

"Well done, good and faithful servant!" the master smiled and said to the second servant. "I will put you in charge of more, as well!"

Then the man who had buried the money he'd been given came to his master. He said, "I knew you would be angry if I lost your money. I was afraid! So I hid your money in the ground. And see? Here is your one talent back."

What do you think the master said when he found out how the third servant managed the talent he'd been given? "WHAT?" roared the master. "You did NOTHING with the money I gave you? At LEAST you could have put it in the bank. It would have earned interest there!" (Interest is the money a bank pays for being able to use the money stored there.) "You are a WICKED and LAZY servant," the master said. "I'm going to give your money to the servant who earned the most for me." **Why did the master take the money away from the servant who buried it?** When the master had given his servants the money, that money was like a loan to them. As good stewards, their job was to use the money as their master would have if he had been there to use it. He expected his money to be used wisely! That's why the master was so upset with the servant who did nothing with the talent he'd been given.

Conclusion

Jesus told this story so that we would all know that God expects us to USE wisely the abilities and gifts that He has given us. It doesn't matter how much or how little we think we have. What's important to God and to us is that we become good stewards, taking care of His gifts through our whole lives and using what He has given us in ways that will please Him.

24 GETTING FOCUSED

Sometimes we might not feel like we're good at doing anything. We might not feel like we have any special gifts, or abilities. But God has given each one of us abilities. As we learn to do new things, we find out more about what we like to do and what we're good at doing.

Use these discussion questions as you lead students in one or more of the Getting Focused activities:

- **What did the first servant do for his master with the money he was given? the second? the third?**

- **What do you think Jesus wanted people to learn from His story of the master and his servants?** (To use the gifts God gives us. Not to be afraid to use the gifts and abilities God gives us.)

- **Who is the master of our lives?** (God.) **What are some ways we can show this?**

- **What are some gifts that God has given you or others you know?** (Money. Ability to make friends. Talent to sing. Opportunities to learn.) **What is a way a kid your age could use that talent or gift for God at school? at home? with your friends?**

- **Think of one gift that God has given you. What are some ways you can be a good steward, or faithful manager, of that gift?** (Bring an offering to church. Sing songs about God. Study and work hard. Don't be lazy. Don't be careless with things.)

- **Tell about a time when someone in the church has helped you or another person. What gifts do you think that person had? In what ways did that person use his or her gifts to help? What were some of the results?**

- **What are some words you might use to encourage other people in God's family to use their gifts?**

ACTIVE FOCUS:
Penny Relay

Materials: Bible with bookmark at Colossians 3:23, discussion questions, spoons, pennies, two unbreakable bowls.

Procedure:

1. **What do you like to do with money?** Volunteers respond. **In our Bible story today, how did two servants use their money wisely? Why was it unwise for the third servant to just bury the master's money?** (Because he could not earn any money for the

© 2000 Gospel Light. Permission to photocopy granted. *The Great Stewardship Adventure for Kids*

master that way.) **Jesus told this story to remind us that God wants us to use the abilities and gifts that He gives us. What are some abilities that God has given you or people you know?**

2. Read Colossians 3:23 aloud. **How does this verse describe the way we should work? What does it mean to work with our whole hearts?** (To work to the best of our abilities. To work cheerfully.) **According to this verse, whom should we be working for in everything we do?** (God.) **Imagine you were talking to the third servant right after he received the money from his master. What might you say about this verse to encourage him to use the money, not bury it?**

3. **Today, we are going to play a game to help us learn Colossians 3:23.** Stand on one side of the room. Place spoons and one bowl with pennies near you. On the other side of the room, students form a line facing you. (If you have a large class, group students into two lines.) Place an empty bowl near students. The first student hops on one foot to you and says the words of Colossians 3:23. Then the student fills spoon with pennies, walks back trying not to spill the pennies and dumps pennies into the bowl. The student may not pick up any pennies that fall to the floor. Continue until each student has had a turn. Students count pennies in bowl. Volunteer from team with the most pennies answers one of the discussion questions. Repeat game as time permits.

Teaching Tips

1. Kids need to be physically active much more often than adults do. It will be much easier for a student to learn a memory verse if he or she can be in motion playing a game at the same time. When regular opportunities for movement are provided, students cooperate more easily during the activities that are primarily listening or sitting activities.

2. Many children will not have Bibles, or those that do may bring a variety of translations. Print verses on a chalkboard, white board or large sheet of paper for all the students to refer to when doing verse activities.

ART FOCUS:
A Picture of Stewardship

Materials: Bible with bookmark at Colossians 3:23, discussion questions, 6-foot (1.8-m) long sheet of butcher paper for each group of two or three students, markers, masking tape.

Preparation: By drawing lines, divide each piece of butcher paper into three sections, each 2 feet (.6 m) long. Print the phrases "The Master Gives," "The Servants Work" and "The Master Returns" as titles, one in each section of the three sheets of butcher paper. Tape each panel to a wall low enough so that students can draw on the paper. (Optional: Tape large sheets of paper to tables. Post pictures on walls when completed.)

Procedure:

1. Divide the class into groups of two or three. Assign one of the servants in the Bible story to

© 2000 Gospel Light. Permission to photocopy granted. *The Great Stewardship Adventure for Kids*

each group. **Each group is going to make a three-frame picture to tell the actions of one of the servants in the three main parts of the story.** Briefly describe the three sections of the story: the master gave talents to the servants; the servants worked or hid the money; finally, the master came back and each servant reported to him what they had done. Each group draws story action from the viewpoint of the servant assigned to them. Encourage students to show the attitudes and actions of the characters in each part of the story. Students may wish to add a summary that tells why they think Jesus would tell people this story.

2. Read Colossians 3:23 aloud. **According to this verse, who should we be working for? What is some of the work you have to do at home? at school? What are some ways you could do it cheerfully with your whole heart?**

3. As students work, ask the discussion questions above. When the illustrations are completed, let the groups briefly tell about their work. Keep the illustrations on the wall of your classroom for the duration of the unit, if possible.

Enrichment Tip

Students cut shapes out of construction paper, fabric and/or foil to glue to illustrations. Materials such as cotton balls, nature objects, fake fur and felt may also be used.

FINAL FOCUS

Stewardship Notes

Materials: Bible with bookmark at Colossians 3:23, class notebook, pen.

Procedure: Show notebook. **This is our class notebook. What do you think we could write in this notebook to help us remember what we've talked about?** (Notes on the ideas we think are important. Prayer requests and answers to prayers.) **Writing down our ideas will help us learn ways to practice stewardship in our everyday lives.**

What did we learn today about being good stewards of God's gifts for our whole lives? Each week, ask a different volunteer to record students' ideas in the class notebook.

Take a few moments to recite Colossians 3:23 together. **According to the verse, what things do we have to do with our whole hearts?** (Everything we do.) **For whom are we working?** (God.)

Ask volunteer to record personal prayer requests students give, adding the date to each request given (recording prayer requests weekly will be an ongoing part of this course). Invite each student to pray a sentence prayer for a request that was given or to thank God for a talent or special ability He has given to any member of the group. Close by asking for God's help in understanding how to be good stewards for Him and asking for His wisdom and strength to use our gifts in ways that please Him.

© 2000 Gospel Light. Permission to photocopy granted. *The Great Stewardship Adventure for Kids*

THE LIVING IT! PAGE

SESSION 1

KEY VERSE

"Whatever you do, work at it with all your heart, as working for the Lord, not for men." Colossians 3:23

The Challenge

Matthew 25:14-30

Jesus told a story about a rich man who gave some talents (money, in this story) to three servants. Follow the path from servant #1 to his money. Write the words you pass (in order) as you go. Do the same for servant #2 and #3. You'll discover what God wants us to learn from this story.

_____

_____

The Super Challenge

The rich man has 22 coins to spend. He can only buy one of the same item. What will he buy?

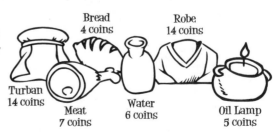

Bread
4 coins

Robe
14 coins

Turban
14 coins

Meat
7 coins

Water
6 coins

Oil Lamp
5 coins

© 2000 Gospel Light. Permission to photocopy granted. *The Great Stewardship Adventure for Kids*

Daily Nuggets

Find out more about being a good steward!

DAY 1 • Ecclesiastes 5:19
What does this verse tell us is a gift from God? What can you do to enjoy and accept what God has given you?

DAY 2 • 1 Thessalonians 2:4
According to this verse, what have we been entrusted with? With whom can you share the good news about Jesus?

DAY 3 • 2 Timothy 3:16,17
What is it that equips us for every good work? What can you do because you know God's Word?

DAY 4 • 1 Corinthians 4:1,2
What does a servant do? What might you do as a servant of Christ?

DAY 5 • Galatians 1:10
As servants of Christ, whose approval do we seek?

Family Builder

You're Doing a Good Job

Ministers, teachers and other people who work for God in your church regularly need support and encouragement because they—like everyone else— sometimes become discouraged. Help your minister, teacher or other worker feel appreciated! Write a family thank-you letter to him or her. Let each family member write a personal note of thanks for some specific thing the person has done for God. Consider baking cookies or drawing a picture of the person hard at work for God and include the treat or drawing with the thank-you letter.

CARING FOR CHEEKS

I already had pets—cats and fish. But my friend Emily had a cockatiel, a soft gray bird with peach-colored cheeks. Cheeks loved to sit on Emily's shoulder and pull at her hair. He was the cutest bird I'd ever seen!

"Cheeks takes a lot of work," Emily told me. "You have to keep the cage clean and feed him fresh foods. I had to buy special bird-safe toys for him. And I have to spend a lot of time with him. It's almost like having a baby around."

Emily let Cheeks ride on my shoulder sometimes. He pulled on my hair with his beak and made little noises by my ear. Because I'd help Emily clean the cage and feed Cheeks, I was sure I knew all about taking care of him. So when Emily's family was going on vacation, she wanted ME to take care of Cheeks. I ran home to tell my mother. This would be SUCH fun!

I got a little less excited when Mom reminded me that we have cats. It would be horrible if Cheeks ended up being their LUNCH! And when I remembered all the things Emily did to take care of Cheeks, I realized I would be doing a lot more than just walking around with Cheeks on my shoulder! But since Emily is my best friend, I decided I would try to take care of Cheeks as if he were my own.

Taking care of Cheeks was a LOT of work! His noises at night would wake me up. And I couldn't even go to my bedroom without Cheeks flapping and chirping to get my attention. He always wanted to play.

When I came home from school one day, one of my cats was sitting RIGHT NEXT to the cage. I was SURE Cheeks was LUNCH! I shooed the cat away. There sat Cheeks, huddled and trembling. I had to talk to him for a long time just to get him to hop onto my finger. When he hopped up onto my shoulder, he crawled inside the front of my shirt as if to say, "I am SO scared! NEVER leave me alone with a cat!"

I felt awful. I was supposed to take care of Cheeks as if he were my own! My best friend had trusted his care to me. But finally Cheeks calmed down. He poked his head out of my shirt and began to tug on my hair. When I knew he was feeling better, I felt better, too. From then on, I was careful to keep the cats out of the house. It was fun to take care of Cheeks while Emily was gone. But the best part was when Emily came to get him; she looked at him and said, "You know, he looks BETTER now than he did when I left. You did a good job!"

I was glad I'd been a good "bird steward." And I don't think I need a bird of my own now. Cheeks is enough for Emily and me, too.

Topic For Conversation with God

When you talk with God this week, complete this sentence prayer: "Thank You, God, that You trust me to take care of _____."

NEXT WEEK: RICHES! What are some things you need?

© 2000 Gospel Light. Permission to photocopy granted. *The Great Stewardship Adventure for Kids*

All We Have Comes From God

LIFE FOCUS

God provides all we need and more.

1 GETTING PREPARED

AIMS

DISCOVER the difference between things we need and things we want;
RECOGNIZE that God gives us all we need and more;
SHOW our thankfulness to God.

SCRIPTURE

John 6:1-15

KEY VERSE

"My God will meet all your needs according to his glorious riches in Christ Jesus."
Philippians 4:19

Teacher's Devotional

Today's story (often referred to as "the feeding of the five thousand") is found in all four gospels. However, John's account explicitly mentions the boy's role in the story. It seems that the boy offered his lunch when the disciples were on their search for food, and Jesus graciously received it. He turned that limited resource into an unlimited picnic—there were even plenty of leftovers!

The great crowd in this incident followed Jesus because of the miraculous signs He was performing. Like most of us, they were drawn to and excited by the spectacular and wondrous. But even though doing wonders wasn't His main purpose, Jesus didn't want to turn them away. He knew the people needed to be with Him, and He knew they were growing hungry. Jesus also knew that His

© 2000 Gospel Light. Permission to photocopy granted. *The Great Stewardship Adventure for Kids*

disciples needed to learn to trust Him to provide what they needed as well and to know that He is the source of great abundance!

We are not much different from that crowd and are quite a bit like those disciples. We not only need to be with Jesus and learn from Him, but we also need to see Him meet our own needs and the needs of others. Then we clearly understand that the burden of providing for those around us doesn't rest with us. It is in the hands of our provider! What He gives us is meant to flow through our hands to those who need it. To move into stewardship, we need to trust Jesus to supply the energy, the means, all we need and more. He is always "able to do immeasurably more than all we ask or imagine" (Ephesians 3:20).

2 GETTING STARTED

Can't Live Without It

Materials: Post-it Notes, markers.

Preparation: Print each of these words or phrases on separate Post-it Notes: "air," "safe place to live," "food," "water," "people who love us," "someone to teach us about God." Hide notes around classroom.

Procedure: Distribute one or two Post-it Notes and a marker to each student. **On your notes, write something that you've been given.** (Allowance. Bike. CD player.) As students finish, they look for and collect hidden Post-it Notes.

Some things we are given are things we need; some are things we want. A need is something that helps keep us alive. A want is something we desire but don't need. Choose two volunteers: a Needs Person and a Wants Person. **One at a time, read items written on Post-it Notes students prepared as well as those you prepared. Decide if the item is something we need or something we want.** Discuss with students items that could be either. For example, we may need shoes, but we don't need the most expensive sneakers in the store. Students place the notes on either the Needs Person or the Wants Person, sticking notes in the areas where a person would actually use the thing written down ("air" near the nose of the Needs Person, etc.).

What are some other things people need? Volunteers answer. **Who provides these things for us? Listen today for a way Jesus proved He can provide all we need and more!**

3 GETTING INTO GOD'S WORD

Materials: Bibles; optional—packages of small round crackers, fish-shaped crackers, small basket.

Preparation: (Optional: Place five round crackers and two fish-shaped crackers in basket. Keep packages of crackers nearby but out of sight.)

Bible Study

Students find John 6 in their Bibles. As you lead the following study, help students to discover answers in their Bibles.

 © 2000 Gospel Light. Permission to photocopy granted. *The Great Stewardship Adventure for Kids*

What's your favorite lunch? How would you feel if someone took your lunch? What might happen if you were the only one who had a lunch and everyone else around you was hungry? Volunteers respond. **Let's find out what happened when there was only one lunch and thousands of hungry people!**

Jesus and His disciples were very tired. Jesus had been healing, praying, teaching and talking for days. The disciples had been working so hard helping all the people who came to see Jesus, they hadn't even had time to eat! So Jesus said, "Let's go by ourselves to a quiet place where we can rest."

Jesus and His disciples got into a boat and rowed across to the far shore of the Sea of Galilee. Since there were no large towns nearby, the disciples thought they could be alone, away from the crowds.

But the disciples got a surprise! **Read John 6:2 to find out who the disciples saw.** They saw hundreds of people! In fact, they saw THOUSANDS!

It seems that when they left Capernaum, some people had seen them go. The news had spread quickly; now, people from towns near and far had left their homes to come see Jesus. There were more than five thousand men, plus their wives and children! **How do you think the tired disciples felt when they saw the crowds of people? What would you have wanted to do in that situation? What do you think Jesus wanted to do?**

Even though Jesus needed some time to rest, He cared so deeply about the people that He took time to teach them and heal them anyway. Jesus had compassion for the people. The word "compassion" means to care deeply enough about another person's needs that you help that person.

Soon it was nearly suppertime. Even though the sun was getting low, the people weren't ready to go home. Nobody wanted to miss anything Jesus was going to say or do! But Jesus' disciples were very tired and hungry. They knew Jesus and all the people were hungry, too. They also knew it would be impossible for all these people to find food to buy for supper! **Read what Jesus said to Philip in John 6:5.** Jesus was concerned about the needs of the hungry crowd, but He already had a plan to take care of them!

"It would take a fortune to feed all these people!" Philip cried.

Jesus must have smiled. He asked His disciples to go through the crowd and find out how much food there was. As Jesus' disciples began asking people if they had food with them, Andrew met a boy with a small basket of food. **Read what Andrew said to Jesus in John 6:8,9. What do you think Jesus might have said to the boy? Why do you think the boy was willing to give up his food?** (Optional: Pass basket containing crackers.)

"Have the people sit down on the grass," Jesus said.

The disciples hurried away to seat the people, while Jesus took the food in His hands. He looked up to heaven and thanked God for the food. Then Jesus began breaking the flat, round loaves of bread and the fish into pieces. The boy who gave his lunch to Jesus must have gasped and rubbed his eyes. His little lunch of five loaves and two fish had GROWN—there were hundreds and HUNDREDS of pieces of bread and fish! (Optional: Add round and fish-shaped crackers to basket, enough so each student may have several. Pass basket and invite students to share the snack.)

Jesus gave the food to each of the disciples to pass out to the people. And no matter how much Jesus gave away, there was always more!

The disciples gave food to every single hungry person. When they finished, many people still had food left. **Read what Jesus said about the leftovers in John 6:12.** The disciples passed baskets around to gather up the extra food. The extra bread and fish filled 12 big baskets! Everyone was amazed! Only God's own Son, Jesus, could take a boy's small lunch and make it into enough food to feed thousands and thousands of people.

© 2000 Gospel Light. Permission to photocopy granted. *The Great Stewardship Adventure for Kids*

The people probably took bread and fish from the baskets for the long walk home. They must have thought about Jesus' great power and how Jesus cared about their needs. He not only gave them what they needed, but He also provided more besides!

Conclusion

The people who followed Jesus that day learned something important. We can depend on God to meet our needs—our physical needs, like hunger, and also our spiritual needs, like needing forgiveness or courage. And He not only gives us what we need, but He also gives us more! We can freely use and share what God gives us like good stewards, because we know He will always take care of us!

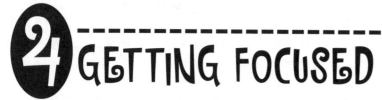

4 GETTING FOCUSED

Use these discussion questions as you lead students in one or more of the Getting Focused activities:

- **What did the people in our story need?** (They needed to learn from Jesus and be healed. They needed food to eat.)

- **In this story, was food a need or a want?** (They had not eaten all day, so it was a need.) **When are times food is a want instead of a need? What kinds of foods would be considered a want instead of a need?**

- **How did Jesus show He cared about the hunger of the people? How did the people know that Jesus could provide even more than they needed?** (There were 12 baskets full of extra food.)

- **How can we know that God will supply all that we need and more?** (He promised that He would and God keeps His promises.)

- **Tell about times when people you know have had physical needs, like food or shelter. How did God meet those needs? How did these people get even more than they needed?**

- **How do we know Jesus cares about each of us? In what ways has God taken care of your needs? In what ways do you have more than you need?**

ACTIVE FOCUS:
Fish Pass

Materials: Bible with bookmark at Philippians 4:19, discussion questions, two beanbags or balls.
Procedure:

1. **Listen to this verse about the things we need.** Read Philippians 4:19 aloud. **What does this verse promise us God will do?** (God gives us all the good things we need.) **In today's story, we learned about a time when Jesus supplied the food people needed and a whole lot more!**

2. Stand with students in a circle. Take a beanbag or ball and give it to the student on your right and say, "This is a fish." Student asks, "A what?" Reply, "A fish." Student then gives the beanbag or ball to the next student and says, "This is a fish." Second student asks, "A what?" First student again

© 2000 Gospel Light. Permission to photocopy granted. *The Great Stewardship Adventure for Kids*

asks you, "A what?" You say, "A fish." This information is passed on to the second student who then passes the beanbag or ball on. Students continue asking and replying.

3. Once the first message is underway, pass another beanbag or ball to the left say, "This is a loaf." Students on the left question and reply in the same manner as those on the right. Students continue passing the two beanbags or balls around the circle until one student ends up holding both.

4. Student with both beanbags or balls tells something that God gives to us or describes a way we can show our thankfulness to God. Ask the discussion questions to help students think of responses and to extend the conversation. Repeat the passing game beginning with different volunteers each time.

Teaching Tips

1. First play a practice game to familiarize the students with the rules and mechanics of the game.

2. Print discussion questions on index cards. On each student's turn, he or she selects a card and answers the question.

Simplification Idea

Play recorded music while passing beanbag or other object around the circle. The student holding the object when the song is stopped answers the question.

ART FOCUS: Thank You, God!

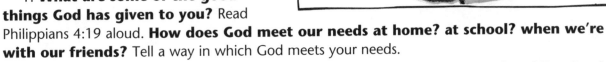

Materials: Bibles, discussion questions, newspaper, small bowls each filled with a couple inches of water, white paper, water-based markers, small paintbrushes.

Preparation: Cover work area with newspaper. Place small bowls of water within students' reach. Make a sample picture following directions below.

Procedure:

1. **What are some of the good things God has given to you?** Read Philippians 4:19 aloud. **How does God meet our needs at home? at school? when we're with our friends?** Tell a way in which God meets your needs.

2. **We have many reasons to thank God! What are some ways people might thank God?** (Prayers, songs, pictures, etc.) Display picture you made. **Today each of you will make something to help you remember to thank God for His gifts.** Distribute paper and markers to students. Students draw pictures and/or write phrases to express their thanks to God for one of the gifts discussed or another object for which they are thankful.

3. Once finished with the markers, students may choose to dip paintbrushes in water and retrace some or all of their work with damp paintbrush. This will blend and blur the colors. Students blot

© 2000 Gospel Light. Permission to photocopy granted. *The Great Stewardship Adventure for Kids*

excess water on newspaper before tracing over their work and to clean the brush before switching colors.

4. As students work, ask the discussion questions to extend the conversation about how God provides all we need and more.

Age-Level Tip

Don't expect every student to display his or her artwork eagerly. For many students this age, artistic expression feels very risky. Many students have had their art ridiculed, effectively choking any desire to be creative. Be sure students know that there is no wrong way to do this project and that every person's work is valuable. When students know that the class is a safe place to express themselves (in art or words), participation increases.

- -

FINAL FOCUS

Stewardship Notes

Materials: Bible with bookmark at Philippians 4:19, class notebook, pen.

Procedure: What did we learn about how God provides for us? Ask a volunteer to record students' answers in the class notebook. Student volunteer reads a few of last week's notes as a review of the previous lesson.

Take a few moments to recite today's key verse, Philippians 4:19. **What does this verse promise God will do? How can this help us to be good stewards?** (We can use everything God gives us, because He provides even more than we need.)

Volunteer opens the class notebook to the prayer journal section. Invite volunteers to give requests or report answers to prayer to be recorded in notebook. **Think of one way that God has given you all you need or more. Let's thank God for those things and anything else for which we might want to thank God.** Lead students to complete the following sentence: "Thank You, God, for . . ." Then invite volunteers to pray aloud for any prayer request from the class notebook. Close by thanking God that He gives us all we need and more.

© 2000 Gospel Light. Permission to photocopy granted. *The Great Stewardship Adventure for Kids*

THE LIVING IT! PAGE

SESSION 2

KEY VERSE

"My God will meet all your needs according to his glorious riches in Christ Jesus." Philippians 4:19

The Challenge →

Philippians 4:19

These papers have gotten all mixed up, but if you write the words from each paper in order on the numbered lines below, you will find the Bible verse.

NEXT WEEK: FAITHFUL! What is a way someone you know is faithful?

© 2000 Gospel Light. Permission to photocopy granted. *The Great Stewardship Adventure for Kids*

Topic for Conversation with God

Dear God, sometimes it's hard to trust You to take care of
_____. Please help me trust You and not worry.

ART BONUS: Draw a picture of a time when God has given you all you need and more!

Daily Nuggets

Because God gives us all we need (and more!), we can surely depend on Him. See if you can discover some words that mean the same thing as the word "depend" in this week's verses.

DAY 1 • 1 John 4:16
"We know and _____ on the love God has for us."

DAY 2 • John 14:1
Jesus said, "Do not let your hearts be troubled. _____ in God; _____ also in me."

DAY 3 • Romans 15:13
Paul prayed that "the God of hope will fill you with all joy and peace as you _____ in him, so that you may overflow with hope by the power of the Holy Spirit."

DAY 4 • Psalm 62:8
"_____ in him at all times, O people; pour out your hearts to him, for God is our refuge."

DAY 5 • 2 Corinthians 1:9
Paul had some hard times, but he said that these things happened so "that we might _____ not on ourselves but on God."

Family Builder

Think of a way you and your family could help supply a need of a family you know. Plan a way to help—then follow your plan!

ONLY OATMEAL

Times weren't easy for the four kids. Their dad was still looking for a job. He'd been unemployed so long, even buying groceries wasn't done very often. Their mother did her best to manage what little money they had so that their clothing, food, and school needs were met. Mom knew that Dad wanted to work. And she knew He loved God and her family very much. Until Dad could bring home a paycheck, she knew the family had to trust God to meet their needs.

The four kids came home from school one day, telling Mom that the school was holding a food drive so that hungry people would have food. They were eager to take some food to give to the poor, just like everyone else. As she looked in the cupboard, Mom saw that the only thing that was still unopened was a small box of oatmeal. Without it, the cupboards were pretty much empty.

Mom took the oatmeal out of the cupboard. She said, "This is all we have, but let's give it to the food drive and see what God does." The Bible said God would supply all their needs. Mom knew He would—she just didn't know exactly HOW God would do it!

The kids were pleased. The next day, they took the small box of oatmeal and happily added it to the other food at the food drive.

That morning, Mom got a phone call. A lady from their church told Mom there was something Mom needed to pick up. So Mom drove to the church. There she looked at what she'd come to pick up—and laughed and cried at the same time as she thought about God's perfect timing. He had kept His promise again! There were several big boxes of food for their family. Mom decided to leave the boxes in the back of the van so that the kids could help her unpack "God's supplies" together!

When the kids came home from school, Mom told them she had a surprise in the van. The kids stared, looking from one big box of food to another. The boxes filled the back of the van! And there, on top of one box was a HUGE box of oatmeal—about three TIMES bigger than the box they had given away! Right there, they thanked God for supplying them with everything they needed—and more besides!

Trusted to Be Faithful

LIFE FOCUS

We can faithfully serve God.

1 GETTING PREPARED

AIMS

DISCOVER that faithful means always being loyal and trustworthy;
RECOGNIZE that because God is faithful to us and we can be faithful;
DISCUSS ways to be faithful stewards of God's gifts.

SCRIPTURE

Genesis 37:12-36; 39—46

KEY VERSE

"Be sure to fear the Lord and serve him faithfully
with all your heart; consider what great things he has done for you." 1 Samuel 12:24

Teacher's Devotional

Joseph was a young man with great potential! His father, Jacob, had given him a coat to indicate he was chosen to be the heir and leader over his brothers. He was given dreams that prepared him for a life of great things. But when his brothers captured him and sold him into slavery, how could all that potential ever manifest itself?

Faithfulness became Joseph's hallmark. As an Egyptian ruler's servant, his potential was realized through his faithfulness. Trusted by his master Potiphar, Joseph was soon put in charge of the entire household. Though he was faithful to that trust, Joseph was falsely accused of wrong-doing and was imprisoned. What did he do in prison? He worked faithfully—and soon became the trustee of the entire operation! Scripture tells us the warden trusted Joseph with everyone held in the prison and made him responsible for all that was done. Joseph was also faithful to the trust of others, interpreting the

© 2000 Gospel Light. Permission to photocopy granted. *The Great Stewardship Adventure for Kids*

cup-bearer's and the baker's dreams and serving faithfully in prison while he waited for release. Finally, after two years had passed, the cup-bearer remembered Joseph's help and recommended him to Pharaoh. Joseph came to Pharaoh with an impressive record not only for dream interpretation but also for faithfulness. And when he was given his high position in Egyptian government? Joseph proved himself faithful!

Your students have great potential as well. But potential can go unrealized unless it is developed and cultivated through faithfulness. How has faithfulness caused you to realize your potential? Think of ways you have learned to be faithful to the service God has given you. What have been the delightful results? When has it been difficult, but God gave you the ability to remain faithful? As you humbly share those stories of God's work in your life, it will make you rejoice. And your students will see that faithful stewardship is found not only in ancient Egypt but also here today!

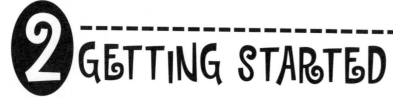

②GETTING STARTED

Faithful Finds

Materials: Construction paper in a variety of colors, markers.

Preparation: Print the following words and phrases in large letters on different colored pieces of construction paper, one word or phrase per piece: "faithful," "loyal," "trustworthy," "Keep promises" and "Do the right thing." Prepare one sheet for each group of two to four students, repeating words and phrases as needed. Tear each sheet into eight to ten pieces. Mix all pieces together.

Procedure: Today we're going to work together to discover the meaning of an important word. Divide class into teams of two to four students each. Assign each team a color of paper pieces. Teams work together to separate their pieces from the other colors and then put their pieces together to discover words. **What does it mean to be faithful?** (Be loyal and trustworthy. Keep promises. Do what's right, even when it's hard.) **Why do you think being faithful is an important part of being a good steward?** Volunteers respond. **Today we're going to hear about how we can be faithful, even when bad things happen!**

③GETTING INTO GOD'S WORD

Materials: Bibles.

Students find Genesis 39 in their Bibles. As you lead the following study, help students to discover answers in their Bibles.

Bible Study

How would you feel if a brother, sister or friend got a better gift than you? Volunteers respond. **Today we're going to hear a story about a boy who had a lot of trouble because his brothers were jealous, especially when he got a special coat from their father.**

Most people would think that Joseph's life was a MESS. When Joseph was probably just a young teenager, his brothers got angry and jealous when their father gave Joseph a beautiful coat made with many different colors. None of them had ever received such a wonderful gift from their father.

© 2000 Gospel Light. Permission to photocopy granted. *The Great Stewardship Adventure for Kids*

Joseph's brothers became so jealous, they attacked him, threw him into a pit and sold him into slavery. Joseph's brothers even told his father that Joseph was dead, so no one would ever come looking for him! Joseph must have been very lonely and afraid. He was taken to a strange country far from home, with no one to talk to or to care about him. But Joseph knew God was with him. He knew God had plans for him. And Joseph chose to be faithful to God and do what was right, even when it wasn't easy.

The man who bought Joseph watched his new slave. **What did Joseph's owner, Potiphar, see? Read Genesis 39:3,4 to find out.** Joseph was a faithful manager of everything his master owned. He was a good steward! But later, Potiphar's wife lied about Joseph and had him unfairly thrown into prison.

Prison in ancient Egypt was NOT a good place to be! But no matter how awful Joseph's life seemed, he still knew that God was with him. He chose to be faithful to God. **Read Genesis 39:21,22 to find out what happened to Joseph in prison.** Once again, Joseph became a trusted manager! He kept on doing what was right. And everyone in the prison respected Joseph.

After Joseph had been in prison for several years, two prisoners asked him to explain strange dreams they had. Joseph did, and he did it correctly, too. A few years after that, someone else asked Joseph's help in interpreting a strange dream: Pharaoh, the king of all Egypt, sent for Joseph!

Pharaoh said, "I've had two dreams and no one can tell me what they mean. I have heard that you can tell the meanings of dreams."

"Tell me about your dreams," Joseph said, "and God will help me know the meaning of them." **What did Pharaoh dream about? Read Genesis 41:17-24.**

Joseph said, "Both dreams mean the same thing. God is telling you that there will be seven years when crops will be plentiful, and then seven years of famine, when no food will grow. God has given you the dreams so that you can prepare for the future."

Pharaoh was impressed. He even asked for Joseph's advice. **What would you do if you knew there was not going to be any way to grow food for a long time?**

"Put a wise man in charge of your kingdom's food supply," Joseph said. "He will need to save grain each year so that during the famine, there will be enough food." Pharaoh thought this was a good idea. In fact, he realized that God was with Joseph. **Read Genesis 41:39,40 to see what Pharaoh did.**

Pharaoh dressed Joseph in fine clothes and jewels. "I will let you rule over the whole land of Egypt," he said. **How do you think Joseph felt about his new position?**

As usual, Joseph took his work seriously. He had plenty of practice at being a faithful steward of other people's things by this time, and Joseph did a GREAT job! He made sure the extra grain that grew during the seven years of plenty was carefully stored. When the famine began, people went to Joseph and bought food. People even came from other countries to buy food.

In fact, the famine was so severe that 10 of Joseph's own brothers came all the way from the land of Canaan to buy food. Joseph's brothers didn't recognize Joseph in his fine clothes, but he recognized them! **Read Genesis 42:8,9 to find out what happened when Joseph saw his brothers.**

Joseph didn't know if his brothers had changed at all. *Are they still the kind of people who would sell one of their family as a slave?* Joseph must have wondered. So Joseph tested them. He put Simeon in prison and told the brothers that Simeon could go free when they brought their youngest brother, Benjamin, to prove they were not spies. The brothers were terrified!

They went back to their father. He was afraid to let his youngest son go. But the food ran out. They HAD to go to Egypt again—with Benjamin.

© 2000 Gospel Light. Permission to photocopy granted. *The Great Stewardship Adventure for Kids*

Joseph kindly invited the brothers to have dinner at his house and released Simeon from prison. But Joseph tested them one more time. Finally, Joseph revealed the truth to his brothers. When they found out the brother they had treated so badly was ALIVE and second only to PHARAOH himself, they were terrified! **Find out what Joseph told his terrified brothers in Genesis 45:7.** Joseph knew that God brought something good out of a bad situation. Later, Joseph's father and brothers and all their families came to live in Egypt, where there was plenty of food. These families lived there for 400 years and became known as the Hebrew people!

Conclusion

Joseph's life didn't turn into the mess people might have expected when his brothers sold him as a slave. Joseph was faithful to obey God and was trustworthy all his life. He was faithful not only to God but also to the men he worked for. And God was faithful to Joseph, rewarding him time and again for his good stewardship. Because God is also faithful to us, we can be like Joseph and faithfully practice good stewardship all of our lives!

GETTING FOCUSED

Use these discussion questions as you lead students in one or more of the Getting Focused activities:

- **Who had the most trouble in today's story?** (Joseph.) **Despite his troubles, to whom did Joseph stay faithful?** (To God. To the men he worked for.)

- **How did God reward Joseph's faithfulness?** (He became an important man with an important job and riches. He was able to help his family and others during the famine.)

- **What things happened to Joseph that might have made him want to give up doing what he knew was right?** (His brothers sold him into slavery. Potiphar's wife lied about him and he was sent to prison.)

- **Why do you think he didn't quit doing what was right?** (He knew God was faithful and would take care of him, so he was faithful to God.)

- **How was Joseph faithful when he worked for Potiphar? What happened as a result of Joseph's faithful service to God and Potiphar?**

- **How was Joseph faithful when he was in prison? Do you think it was hard or easy? How did being faithful make a difference in his life? in Pharaoh's life? in the life of Joseph's family?**

- **How do you think Joseph knew God was with him? How did that help him keep on being faithful?**

- **When are some times kids your age might want to quit doing what is right and just give up?**

- **How do we know that God will help us every day? What do we need to do to be faithful people like Joseph?**

 © 2000 Gospel Light. Permission to photocopy granted. *The Great Stewardship Adventure for Kids*

ACTIVE FOCUS:
Stewardship Scenes

Materials: Bibles, discussion questions.

Preparation: Clear an area of your room of furniture so that it can be used as a stage.

Procedure:

1. Read, or ask a volunteer to read, 1 Samuel 12:24 aloud. **What does this verse tell us to be sure to do? What are we to consider?**

2. Divide class into groups of two to four students each. Ask each group to think secretly of a situation in which someone might act faithfully to take care of someone else's belongings. Give help to groups by asking questions such as, **When might a kid take care of something for someone else at school? during the summer? in a family?** Allow groups several minutes to plan (and practice, if possible) their pantomimes. Be available to help students as needed.

3. Each group takes a turn to act out the situation (without using words) for other groups to guess (feeding the class fish, walking a neighbor's dog, doing the dishes after dinner, etc.). After each situation is identified, actors answer one of the discussion questions as a team.

Teaching Tips

1. If students pause during their pantomimes, ask a question or two to help them remember the action or think of what to do next.

2. While asking questions and in other conversation with students, avoid making assumptions regarding family. Include references to children who live in a blended family and/or who visit their other parents.

Discipline Tip

In handling misbehavior in your classroom, use sentences that build bridges between you and your students, rather than create barriers. For example, **Mario, I really want you to enjoy being in our class. I think you'll have a good time doing these scenes if you pay attention while the other groups are acting their scenes out. Your turn will be next.**

ART FOCUS:
Colorful Cloth Collages

Materials: Bibles, discussion questions, construction paper, a variety of collage materials (fabric, thread, yarn, ribbon, etc.), glue, scissors.

Procedure:

1. Read, or ask a volunteer to read, 1 Samuel 12:24. **Joseph is a good example of someone who was a faithful steward and served God with all his heart. What reason does our verse give for serving the Lord faithfully?** (Because of the great things God has done for us.) **In our story today, we learned Joseph was given a coat of colorful cloth. Let's practice stewardship by making collages from**

© 2000 Gospel Light. Permission to photocopy granted. *The Great Stewardship Adventure for Kids*

colorful cloth and other materials for each other.

2. Students select construction paper and other materials to be used in a collage. Then students divide into pairs and exchange materials with their partners. **You are being trusted with your partner's collage materials. Show your faithful stewardship by creating the best collage you can for your partner.**

3. Students create collages by cutting and gluing materials to construction paper. Encourage students to experiment by cutting fabric into a variety of shapes, by gluing yarn or thread designs onto fabric pieces and by braiding ribbon or yarn before adding to collage. Students may ask each other for ideas or preferences as they create each other's collages, but make sure comments remain positive and noncritical.

4. As students work, ask the discussion questions for volunteers to answer. When finished, students give collages to their partners to take home as reminders that God wants us to be faithful stewards of His gifts.

Teaching Tips

1. Instead of using construction paper, cut vests from paper grocery bags. Students glue collage materials onto the vests.

2. Instead of using suggested materials, students tear shapes from construction paper, newsprint, wrapping paper and magazine pictures. Students glue shapes as the "fabric" on their collages.

3. On a large sheet of butcher paper, draw a large coat outline. Students fill in coat outline with collage materials.

- -

FiNAL FOCUS

Stewardship Notes

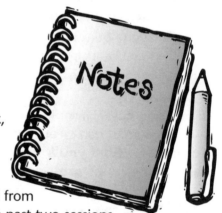

Materials: Bible with bookmark at 1 Samuel 12:24, class notebook, pen.

Procedure: What did we learn about being faithful stewards today? Volunteer records students' responses in class notebook. After students have given answers, volunteer reads aloud from the class notebook a few important points students gave during the past two sessions. **What are some of the things you are learning about stewardship in this course?** Volunteers respond.

Take a few moments to recite today's key verse, 1 Samuel 12:24, together. **What two things does this verse tell us we are to be sure to do?** (Fear the Lord and serve Him faithfully.) **Why should we do these things?** (Because of the great things God has done for us.). Talk with interested students about the greatest thing God has done for us: sending His Son, Jesus, to be our Savior (see "Leading a Student to Christ" on p. 111).

Volunteer opens the class notebook to the prayer journal section. Invite volunteers to give requests or report answers to prayer to be written in class notebook. Volunteer reviews some of the requests from previous weeks. Invite students to pray silently, asking God's help to faithfully serve Him. Close by praying aloud for prayer requests from the class prayer journal and thanking God for all the great things He has done for us.

© 2000 Gospel Light. Permission to photocopy granted. *The Great Stewardship Adventure for Kids*

KEY VERSE

"Be sure to fear the Lord and serve him faithfully with all your heart; consider what great things he has done for you."
1 Samuel 12:24

SESSION 3

THE LIVING IT! PAGE

Genesis 37; 41—45
Unscramble the names of Joseph's brothers. (Hint: Read Genesis 35:23-26.) Then choose one brother and draw a line to link him with the brother with the same ID number. Link all the brothers, being careful not to cross any lines when forming your links!

The Challenge

The Super Challenge

Take the circled letters in the names to spell out the important trait that Joseph showed when dealing with his brothers.

_ _ _ _ _ _ _ _ =

 (4)

Ⓘ E L V

 (1)

Ⓞ E H J S E P

 (2)

A D Ⓝ

 (2)

B U L Z U N E

 (4)

A H S A Ⓒ R I Ⓢ

 (5)

Ⓐ D G

 (1)

H A Ⓢ R E

 (3)

E Ⓞ S I N M

 (6)

H A U J D

 (3)

E I J Ⓜ N B N A

 (6)

B E R E N U

 (5)

H Ⓟ A I N L T A

Topic for Conversation with God

Dear God, sometimes it is really hard to stick with some jobs I have to do. Please help me do ____ ____ faithfully.

© 2000 Gospel Light. Permission to photocopy granted. *The Great Stewardship Adventure for Kids*

Daily Nuggets

Check out these verses to learn how some great Bible guys were able to serve God faithfully!

DAY 1: Joseph
After being sold as a slave, wrongfully accused and going to jail, where did Joseph end up? (Read Genesis 41:37-40.)

DAY 2: Moses
In Exodus 14, Moses was leading the Israelites to the Red Sea when Pharaoh and his men put them in a hard spot. Read verses 13-18 to see how Moses (and God!) showed their faithfulness.

DAY 3: David
In 1 Samuel 17, Israel was in a tight spot—Goliath threatened them every day! When David decided to take on Goliath, what did he say about this threat of a giant and how God would be faithful? (Read verses 34-37.)

DAY 4: Elisha
What happened when some men in 2 Kings 2:19-22 asked Elisha for some good water? How did Elisha show faithfulness to God? To whom did Elisha give credit for making the water good?

DAY 5: Peter
Some people thought Peter was talking about Jesus too much and they decided putting him in jail would keep him quiet. Read Acts 12:5-17 to find out what happened instead. Who was faithful in this story?

NEXT WEEK: CREATION! What are some ways people you know take care of God's world?

Profiting from Plumeria

Josh and his little brother, Jordan, lived in a small tourist village in Hawaii. It was a great place to live, but the boys seldom had any money. Josh liked to think of ways to make money—his mom said it was one of his talents. So he began planning a business. He and Jordan could earn money of their own!

Josh couldn't wait to tell his mom about his newest plan! He found his mom in the yard and said, "Mom! I have a GREAT idea for making money!"

Mom looked up. Josh began to tell her his plan as fast as he could. First, there was a big plumeria tree growing nearby that always had fragrant white blossoms—perfect for making leis! They could make leis and sell them to the tourists.

Mom began to smile. What a mind Josh had! Her boys might make some money with this business. And she could see they would also learn lessons about faithfully following plans and being dependable! She ruffled Josh's hair and said, "It's worth a try! Let's get started!"

She helped Josh and Jordan find heavy thread and big needles. With an old broomstick for a pole, the boys had all they needed! They picked flowers, made leis, strung them on their pole and carried the pole on their shoulders to a place where they could stand where lots of tourists walked by and shopped.

Josh was right. The tourists loved buying the leis! But some days sales were poor, so the boys began to save money to make up for the slow days. Sometimes they bought cereal or bread to help Mom with the grocery bill. Some money went into the collection plate at Sunday School. And sometimes when they counted the money, they gave a little away to another kid or bought ice cream for a friend.

Once the shop owners knew about J and J Enterprises, they would tell the boys when they were on time and dependable, they usually sold all their leis!

As time went on, Josh and Jordan grew more able to manage time and money. They learned to be dependable. As grown men, Josh and Jordan no longer make leis, but they still work together on some of their big business ideas. And it all started with a plumeria tree, some needles and thread and a pole—and the result was more kinds of profit than simply making money!

© 2000 Gospel Light. Permission to photocopy granted. *The Great Stewardship Adventure for Kids*

Earth and All Belong to God

LIFE FOCUS

We need to care for all of God's creation.

① GETTING PREPARED

AIMS

DISCUSS how everything belongs to God because He made it;
RECOGNIZE how people can take care of God's creation;
PLAN a way to care for God's creation.

SCRIPTURE

Genesis 2:4-25; 3

KEY VERSE

"The earth is the Lord's, and everything in it, the world, and all who live in it;
for he founded it upon the seas and established it upon the waters." Psalm 24:1,2

Teacher's Devotional

We, the members of the human race, pretty much think we own the Earth. Many of us even make mortgage payments to ensure ownership of a little piece of it. On a grander scale, nations often go to war over ownership of large portions of the globe; however, God's view of human life and its relationship to His planet are not quite the same!

The narrative of Genesis 2 gives us more insight into some aspects of creation than does the narrative in the first chapter. Chapter two further describes the pristine terrain and details the creation of the first man and woman. The amazing richness of God's creation, Adam and Eve's

© 2000 Gospel Light. Permission to photocopy granted. *The Great Stewardship Adventure for Kids*

work to take care of His creation, and the simple intimacy of God's love made life for these first humans paradise in the truest sense of the word.

This narrative also gives us direction about our own work as stewards of God's creation. We are, as was Adam, to follow God's direction to work it and take care of it (see Genesis 2:15). This lesson is a good place to begin working the implications of that verse into our daily lives. God's world is a gift to be respected, not a disposable resource.

As your students understand that God created and owns everything and that He gives humans the job of caring for the Earth, they will see how stewardship is actually a privilege given by God. It is because we are created in the image of God (see Genesis 1:27) that we can be part of God's creation in a way that brings glory to Him.

GETTING STARTED

Created or Invented?

Materials: Living plant(s), toy car, kitchen utensil, calculator (or other electronic device).

Preparation: Make sure batteries work in objects that need them.

Procedure: Display items you brought and ask students to describe each in turn. **What can you tell about the (toy car)? How is it different from the (plant)?** Pass small items around class. (Optional: Meet outside. Include the sky, dirt, rocks, etc. in discussion.)

Discuss the difference between something made by God and something made by people:

• **How do you think people got the idea to make a car?**

• **Why do you think someone thought to make a computer?**

• **Do any of you know an inventor? Tell about him or her and the things he or she has invented.**

• **What did God create? What have people invented from what God created?**

Why do you think people are able to invent new things? (Because God gives people intelligence.) **If God created everything used to make inventions and gave people the intelligence needed, who do you think really owns the things people invent? These new things belong to God, too! Listen today to learn ways we can use and take care of God's creation.**

GETTING INTO GOD'S WORD

Materials: Bibles.

Bible Study

Students find Genesis 2 in their Bibles. As you lead the following study, help students to discover answers in their Bibles.

Have you ever made anything out of mud? What happened to it? Today we'll find out what God did with a little bit of dirt.

 © 2000 Gospel Light. Permission to photocopy granted. *The Great Stewardship Adventure for Kids*

Near the end of the sixth day of God's work creating the world, it was no longer dark and empty. Now the world was filled with growing plants. Animals of all kinds ran and jumped; colorful, flying birds flew through the air and fish swam through the waters. The sun shone in the daytime and the moon and stars at night. It was all brand-new and beautiful. But there was still more to do.

God said, "Let us make a human in our image, in our likeness, to rule and take care of the world I have made."

What did God do? Read Genesis 2:7 to find out. God took dirt from the ground. He used the dirt to form a human body. THEN God breathed His breath into the body. And that body became a LIVING PERSON! Only God could do that! God named that person Adam. Adam's name sounds like the word in his language for "dirt" because he had been made from the earth.

God had planted a beautiful garden that He called Eden. **Read Genesis 2:9 to learn what was in the garden.** Out of this beautiful garden ran a river that divided into four other rivers. This was an amazing place! And into this wonderful place, God put Adam to live.

God gave Adam some important work to do. **What work do you think the first man did? Read Genesis 2:15 to find out.** God had other exciting work for Adam, too. Besides taking care of the garden, God gave Adam the job of naming all the animals. God brought every animal to Adam and let Adam give each animal its name.

But as Adam named the animals, he probably realized he was ALONE. Out of all the animals God had created, there was no animal suited to be a partner or friend just right for Adam. There was no one around who could talk with Adam or be a companion to him. Dogs were nice and giraffes were a lot of fun, but there was no one just like Adam. **Read Genesis 2:18 to find out what God thought about Adam being alone.** Of course, God had known all along that it wasn't good for Adam to be alone. Now Adam must have known it, too.

What did God do for Adam? Read Genesis 2:21,22. God made Adam fall asleep. Then He opened up Adam's side and gently took a rib out of Adam's side. He closed up the place again while Adam continued to sleep. And from that rib, God formed ANOTHER person! And into that person, God breathed life, too. Only God could do that!

God brought this person to Adam. Can you imagine how surprised Adam was? This person was human, with arms and legs and a head and a smile, but she wasn't JUST like Adam. She was female. Here was another person—one who was a perfect match for him! **What did Adam say about this person? Learn by reading Genesis 2:23.** Later, Adam named the woman Eve. In Adam's language, "Eve" probably means "living," and Adam chose this name because she would be the mother of all living people. So Adam and Eve worked together, taking care of the beautiful garden God gave them to live in.

Conclusion

Because God made the world and everything in it, the Earth and everything in it belong to Him. And it's part of our work as God's good stewards to care for, enjoy and use the beautiful world He has given us.

© 2000 Gospel Light. Permission to photocopy granted. *The Great Stewardship Adventure for Kids*

24 GETTING FOCUSED

Use these discussion questions as you lead students in one or more of the Getting Focused activities:

- **What was the special job God gave to Adam?** (To take care of the plants and animals in the garden.) **Do you think it was easy or hard to name all the animals? Why or why not?**

- **Why do you think God created plants? birds? humans?**

- **If you were Adam or Eve, what would you have liked about living in the beautiful garden God made for you? What do you think you would like best about caring for a beautiful garden like Eden?**

- **What are some ways people don't take good care of the creation God has given us?**

- **What are ways a kid your age can care for God's creation? How can you care for the place in His creation where God has put you?**

- **Where do people get the intelligence to invent things? Where do people get the materials they need to invent things?** Guide students to see that even when people invent things, the intelligence and materials needed come from God, so even our inventions belong to God.

ACTIVE FOCUS:
Alphabetical Creation

Materials: Bible with bookmark at Psalm 24:1,2; discussion questions; large sheets of paper; markers; masking tape.

Preparation: Print the alphabet down one side of large sheet of paper, preparing one paper for each group of up to eight students. Use masking tape to make a starting line on one side of the room. Tape alphabet papers to wall opposite masking-tape line. Place markers on floor under alphabet papers.

Procedure:

1. Read Psalm 24:1,2 aloud. **What does this verse tell us belongs to God?** (The earth and everything in it.) **Let's play a game to help us plan different ways to care for God's creation.**

2. Divide class into teams of up to eight students each. Teams line up behind starting line. Each team sends one person at a time to its large sheet of paper to write a name of something God made next to the letter of the alphabet with which the word begins. Teams attempt to name something that begins with each letter of the alphabet. Call time after several minutes.

3. Teams take turns choosing one creation at a time from their paper and discussing it. **Why do you think God created this? What is a way we could take care of or use this creation?**

© 2000 Gospel Light. Permission to photocopy granted. *The Great Stewardship Adventure for Kids*

Teams continue taking turns as time allows. **What is a way you could take care of something God created? What is something you could take care of this week? every day?**

Enrichment Ideas

1. Students vary the way they move across the room according to your directions. Students might crawl, skip, hop on one foot, walk backwards, etc.

2. For a greater challenge, students must list creations according to alphabetical order.

Age-Level Tip

The reading, writing and spelling abilities of fourth, fifth and sixth graders can vary drastically. When putting students in groups, make sure to include at least one good reader and/or writer in each group. And don't worry about spelling—the most important part of this activity is understanding we are to care for God's creation. However, If possible, carry a small package of self-adhesive notes and a pencil with you. Then if a student asks you how to spell a word, you can write it down quickly and keep the activity moving.

ART FOCUS:
Recyclable Art

Materials: Bible with bookmark at Psalm 24:1,2; discussion questions; a variety of unbreakable recyclable and/or craft materials (soda cans, craft sticks, cardboard tubes, toothpicks, aluminum foil, egg cartons, Styrofoam pieces, straws, string, paper, etc.); scissors; glue; masking tape; markers.

Procedure:

1. Read Psalm 24:1,2 aloud. **This verse tells us that the earth and everything in it belong to God. What else does the verse tell us belongs to God?** (Everyone on the earth.) **God wants us to take care of His creation and each other. What are some ways you can care for God's creation?** As volunteers tell answers (water plants, pick up trash, feed birds, etc.), ask, **What kind of object could you make that would remind you to do that job?** (A flower, a trash can, a bird, etc.)

2. Each student uses recyclable materials to make one of the objects discussed to serve as a reminder of a way to take care of God's creation. Students may use markers to add details or decoration.

3. To extend the conversation about planning ways to care for God's creation, ask discussion questions as students work.

Teaching Tips

1. If craft and recyclable materials are not available, students may draw pictures of objects that remind them to care for God's creation.

2. Sit with students, joining them in the activity and making an object yourself. Avoid hovering over children or moving mysteriously behind them. Simply working alongside students helps foster positive relationships.

drinking straw

egg carton section

soda can

FINAL FOCUS

Stewardship Notes

Materials: Bible with bookmark at Psalm 24:1,2; class notebook; pen.

Procedure: What did we learn about caring for God's creation today? Ask a volunteer to record students' responses in the class notebook. After students have given answers, ask volunteer to read aloud from the class notebook a few points students gave in the previous lessons, without telling from which lesson they came. Invite students to tell the key verse or Bible story associated with each statement read aloud.

Read aloud today's key verse, Psalm 24:1,2. **What does this verse tell us belongs to God? What reason does this verse give for why everything belongs to God?**

Volunteer opens the class notebook to the prayer journal section. Volunteers may tell requests or report answers to prayer as notes are taken. After students have given prayer requests, invite students to pray silently, asking God to show them each a way to care for His creation. Close the session with a "popcorn prayer" time. Invite each student to pray a short sentence prayer for one of the prayer requests, a prayer of praise to God for all the beautiful things He has created or a prayer of thanks to God for allowing us to care for His creation.

© 2000 Gospel Light. Permission to photocopy granted. *The Great Stewardship Adventure for Kids*

THE LIVING IT! PAGE

SESSION 4

KEY VERSE

"The earth is the Lord's, and everything in it, the world, and all who live in it; for he founded it upon the seas and established it upon the waters."
Psalm 24:1,2

Genesis 1:26-31

The Challenge →

God created Adam and Eve and gave them the Garden of Eden to live in. Unscramble the words on each insect, and then write the word from each one below the matching insect at the bottom of the page. You'll find out why God created Adam and Eve and you!

NEXT WEEK: TREASURE! What is something you treasure? Why?

© 2000 Gospel Light. Permission to photocopy granted. *The Great Stewardship Adventure for Kids*

Choose one of the "Planetary Care!" ideas on this page and do it as a family!

Family Builder

Discovery and Exploration

Take your family on a walk or bike ride. Identify as many things as you can that God created—in alphabetical order! Then play the same game using things you see that are made by humans. How have those human inventions been used to care for (or hurt) God's creation?

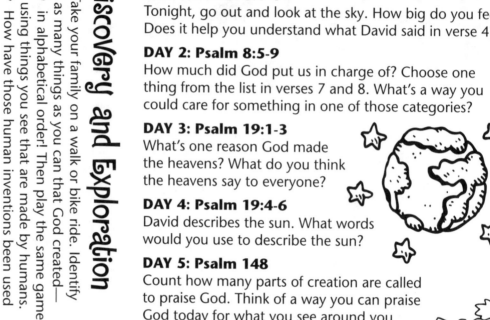

Daily Nuggets

Let's look at Psalms for some descriptions of God's big gift of our home planet!

DAY 1: Psalm 8:1-4
Tonight, go out and look at the sky. How big do you feel? Does it help you understand what David said in verse 4?

DAY 2: Psalm 8:5-9
How much did God put us in charge of? Choose one thing from the list in verses 7 and 8. What's a way you could care for something in one of those categories?

DAY 3: Psalm 19:1-3
What's one reason God made the heavens? What do you think the heavens say to everyone?

DAY 4: Psalm 19:4-6
David describes the sun. What words would you use to describe the sun?

DAY 5: Psalm 148
Count how many parts of creation are called to praise God. Think of a way you can praise God today for what you see around you. Then do it!

PLANETARY CARE!

We've probably all heard these words: "If you'd had to WORK to get that (game, bike, toy), you'd take better CARE of it!"

Well, there's one gift we've ALL been given (and judging by the way we've taken care of it, it's easy to see we didn't have to work for it!). The gift? Our planet Earth! The giver? God!

Now some of you may be thinking, Care for the Earth? Sounds like WORK! It's BORING!

Negative. Nope. No way! Caring for and appreciating this big gift can be a lot of FUN!

HOW ABOUT THESE IDEAS?

• Make up a trash scavenger-hunt list for you and your friends. (Divide a park into team areas. Compete to see who gets everything on the list!)
• Secretly rake leaves for an elderly neighbor. (It's a blast to see your neighbor try to figure out who'd do such a thing!)
• Pick up trash when you go to the beach or park. (Make it a game—you can only pick up what's right in your path!)
• Adopt a creek or park where you often play. (Take a trash bag with you every once in a while; get your friends to help fill it!)
• Make something cool from recyclable stuff. Show it off at school!
• Start a garden in which you plant vegetables you can give to a food bank.
• Do a science project on recycling or a way to use energy more efficiently.

To get even more ideas, write or e-mail an organization that helps people care for the environment.

Topic for Conversation with God

Dear God, thank You for making _____. Help me think of ways to help take care of what You have made.

© 2000 Gospel Light. Permission to photocopy granted. *The Great Stewardship Adventure for Kids*

Treasure Trove

LIFE FOCUS

We can give cheerfully of our treasures:
time, talents, money and possessions.

1 GETTING PREPARED

AIMS

DISCOVER four kinds of treasure we can all give to God and to help others;
COMPARE different attitudes about giving;
IDENTIFY different ways to give to God.

SCRIPTURE

Mark 10:17-22; 12:41-44.

KEY VERSE

"Each one should give what he has decided in his heart to give, not reluctantly
or under compulsion, for God loves a cheerful giver." 2 Corinthians 9:7

Teacher's Devotional

The gospel incidents of the poor widow and the rich young ruler are studies in contrast. With no
prospects at all, the widow gave all she had. But the prospects of future power and position colored
the wealthy young man's thinking. He hesitated; then he walked away. He knew he could never give
up all he had to follow Jesus. We'd like to think we'd be like the poor widow who was left with nothing but her simple trust in God. However, we may all be far more like that rich young man than we
imagine.

   As stewards, we choose every day to give all at the feet of our provider in trust or to walk away,
knowing we have what we're tightly clutching but little else besides. As we learn, however, that
nothing is really ours to possess—not our lives, not our time, not our talent, not our treasure—we
can relax our grip, realizing not only that God is able to provide but also that He always has something better for us—as soon as we stop clutching and hesitating and allow Him to fill our hands and
hearts!

   Think of ways God has richly blessed you when you have given to Him. Share those stories with

© 2000 Gospel Light. Permission to photocopy granted. *The Great Stewardship Adventure for Kids*

your students. It may not be a story about money. It may be about time, talent or that thing you thought you could never live without. Your stories will vividly illustrate this truth: God tells us that as we delight ourselves in Him and make Him our treasure, He will not only give us all we need but will also fulfill the desires of our hearts (see Psalm 3:4,5)!

② GETTING STARTED

Hidden Treasures

Materials: A variety of colored construction paper, marker, scissors, balloons.

Preparation: Print the following words on different colors of construction paper: "time," "talents," "money" and "possessions." Cut each word paper into two puzzle pieces. Repeat words as necessary so that there is at least one puzzle piece for each student. Roll up puzzle pieces so that they are small enough to fit in balloon. Put each puzzle piece inside a separate balloon, inflate balloon and knot it closed.

Procedure: When I say the word "treasure," what do you think of? Volunteers respond. **In these balloons are hidden treasures, pieces of a puzzle. Put the pieces of the puzzle together to discover what the treasures are.** Students pop balloons to find pieces of construction paper and then team up with students who have the same color of paper. Students put the pieces together to discover the words "time," "talent," "money" and "possessions." **How is the word you discovered a treasure?** Volunteers respond. **Today we'll talk about how we get these treasures and how good stewards can give them to God.**

③ GETTING INTO GOD'S WORD

Materials: Bibles.

Bible Study

Students open their Bibles to Mark 10. As you lead the following study, help students to discover answers in their Bibles.

Today we're going to talk about two people with very different attitudes about what they treasured. In fact, you could say their treasures were very different. See if you can tell what the difference was.

Jesus had been teaching and talking all day long. Everyone wanted to see and hear this famous teacher! But finally, Jesus turned to leave town and get some rest.

As he left, a young man came up to Jesus and dropped to his knees. Anyone could see the young man was rich. His expensive coat flapped around his ankles. He probably wore rings that glinted in the afternoon sun. The young man had been listening to Jesus teach people about God's wonderful love. Now he had an important question to ask.

"Good teacher," the rich young man asked, "what do I have to do to live forever?" **What do you think Jesus told him? Read Mark 10:19 to see.**

Now the young man ALWAYS tried to do what was right. He ALWAYS obeyed the commandments—at least he thought he did.

© 2000 Gospel Light. Permission to photocopy granted. *The Great Stewardship Adventure for Kids*

"I've obeyed every one of those commandments since I was a little boy!" the young man exclaimed. "What else must I do?"

"You only need to do one thing," Jesus said. Imagine the young man's excitement—only ONE thing? Maybe the young man was expecting Jesus to give him another rule to obey.

But Jesus knew that the young man's riches were the most important things in his life. He loved all the things he owned more than he loved God.

What did Jesus do? What did He say? Read Mark 10:21 to find out. Jesus cared about this young man. The Bible says He looked at and loved the young man! Jesus knew what the young man needed. Gently Jesus said, "Sell everything you own and give it to the poor. Then come and follow Me."

The young man's face fell. *How can Jesus ask me to sell all my treasures and give the money to other people?* he may have wondered.

What did the young man do? Why? Read Mark 10:22. Sadly the young man turned and walked away from Jesus. He decided he just couldn't do what Jesus asked. He treasured his money and things more than he treasured God.

Now let's turn to Mark 12. Jesus and His disciples were standing in the Temple across from where people put money into the offering boxes.

In Bible times when people worshiped God at the Temple in Jerusalem, they brought their money gifts to one area where there were big offering boxes. On the tops of the boxes were metal horns, like the big end of a tuba. People dropped their coins down these horns and into the box.

As Jesus and His friends sat and watched, many people passed through and dropped their money into the offering boxes. Some of the people who came to give were very rich. They took handfuls of valuable coins out of their big money bags. Perhaps they glanced around to see if others noticed how much money they gave, and then they dropped their money into the horn, making a lovely loud sound, coins clanking and chinking their way down the horn and into the box. **How do you think these rich people felt about themselves?**

As Jesus and His friends watched, a very poor widow walked to an offering box. Because she was a widow, she had no one to care for her and very little money. **What did the poor woman do? Read Mark 12:42.** The woman didn't have a big bag of money. In fact, she didn't need a bag, for she had only two little coins. The coins were so TINY that both of them together were worth less than one of our pennies.

The poor widow quietly dropped both of those tiny coins in the offering box and walked away. **How much noise do you think those coins made as they went down into the offering box?**

Of course, Jesus knew all about the poor widow. He knew that those two little coins were ALL the money she had. When she gave her last two coins as a love gift to God, she had no more money. And she probably didn't have much of a chance to earn more money. **Why do you think the widow gave all her money?**

When Jesus saw what the widow gave, He called His disciples to Him. **What did He say? Read Mark 12:43 to find out.**

How surprised Jesus' friends must have been! What could Jesus mean? **How could the poor woman's coins be worth more than all the money the others put in? Let's read Jesus' explanation in verse 44.**

All the other people still have plenty of money left for themselves. But this woman gave ALL the money she had.

Conclusion

The rich young man's reaction to Jesus showed where his treasure was. Though he loved God, he treasured his money more. The poor widow showed what she treasured, too. She loved God so much, she gave up ALL her money. God doesn't require us to give up everything we have, like Jesus told the young man to do or like the poor widow did. God wants us to be sure to not let our money or possessions or anything else get in the way of loving and serving God. Because we treasure God above everything else, we cheerfully give to God not only our money but also our other possessions, time and talents!

24 GETTING FOCUSED

It's easy to think that someone who gives a lot of money to church must be very important to God. But in God's eyes the size of a gift doesn't matter. Whether gifts are small or large, Jesus wants us to know that what's most important to God is the attitude we have when we give to Him. Giving cheerfully, out of love and gratefulness, is what counts in His eyes!

Use these discussion questions as you lead students in one or more of the Getting Focused activities:

- **In our story today, what was hard for the rich young man to do?**
- **What would giving up his money have really shown about the young man?** (That he loved God.)
- **What do the rich young man's actions tell us about him?** (His money was more important to him than God.)
- **How were the rich young man and the rich people who put their money into the offering box at the Temple alike?**
- **What do the poor widow's actions tell us about her?** (She loved God so much that she gave everything she had to Him. She trusted God to take care of her if she gave Him her money.)
- **How would you describe the widow? How was she different from the other people putting money in the offering boxes?**
- **Why was the widow's offering more pleasing to God?**
- **What are ways someone your age could show that God is more important than money or possessions?**
- **How could you be a cheerful giver at home? at school? at the park?**

ACTIVE FOCUS:
Penny Pitch

Materials: Bible with bookmark at 2 Corinthians 9:7, discussion questions, paper, marker, four metal bowls or pie tins, masking tape, pennies.

Preparation: Print the following words on four pieces of paper, one word or phrase per paper: "time," "talents," "money" and "possessions." Place papers in bowls arranged as shown in sketch.

© 2000 Gospel Light. Permission to photocopy granted. *The Great Stewardship Adventure for Kids*

Lay a masking-tape line about 5 feet (1.5 m) from the bowls.

Procedure:

1. Show papers you prepared. **These are different kinds of gifts people give to God. How can we give these kinds of gifts to God?** (Giving time to God by reading the Bible or praying. Giving of our talents by singing songs of praise to God or helping someone with their homework. Giving money to the church or to people who need it. Giving possessions by sharing what we have with others who don't have as much.) **Let's play a game to name as many different ways to give as we can.**

2. Give each student an equal number of pennies. Students stand behind masking-tape line and take turns tossing the pennies into the bowls. When a penny lands in a bowl, student tells a way to give to God a gift in the category described on the paper in the bowl. Or student may choose to answer a discussion question. Mix bowls around between each round of play.

3. After several rounds, invite a student to find and read aloud 2 Corinthians 9:7. **What does this verse say we should do? What does this verse say our attitude should be when we give? Why do you think the way we feel or think about what we give is important? Why do you think a good steward is able to give cheerfully?** (He or she knows God is the source of what we have. It all belongs to God anyway.)

4. Continue as time permits. Tell students a way you plan to give to God during the week. Invite students to tell ways they plan to give to God and encourage them to follow through on their plans.

Table Option

Place bowls in middle of table. Students sit in chairs around table and take turns tossing pennies while remaining seated.

Enrichment Ideas

1. The larger and deeper the bowl, the easier to toss the penny in without it bouncing out. Bring bowls of different sizes and depths and switch them periodically to increase the challenge.

2. Include a fifth bowl with "discussion question" written on a piece of paper inside it. When a student's penny lands in this bowl, student answers a discussion question.

ART FOCUS:
Gift Quilt

Materials: Bible with bookmark at 2 Corinthians 9:7, discussion questions, 12-inch (30-cm) construction paper squares in a variety of colors, used magazines, scissors, glue, markers, tape.

Procedure:

1. Read 2 Corinthians 9:7 aloud. **According to this verse, how much are we supposed to give to God?** (However much we decide to give.) **What attitude should we have when we give to God?** (Cheerful, not reluctant or feeling like we have to.) **When we think about giving to God cheerfully, it's good to think about the different ways we can give. We're going to make a quilt of many different colors to show different ways to give to God!**

2. Each student chooses two different-colored paper squares. On one square, student glues pictures of different types of treasures cut or torn from magazines. (Optional: Students draw items

© 2000 Gospel Light. Permission to photocopy granted. *The Great Stewardship Adventure for Kids*

they want to include but can't find in magazines.) Encourage students to include a variety of different kinds of ways to spend our time, talents, money or objects.

3. On the second square, each student draws or writes ways to give these gifts to God. As students work, ask the discussion questions to extend the conversation and to help them think of different ways to give to God.

4. Students write their names on their squares. Guide students to tape squares together to form a quilt-like pattern (see sketch). Display in hallway or other prominent area at your church.

Alternative Ideas

1. Instead of taping quilt squares together, glue them onto a large sheet of butcher paper or poster board.

2. Provide one or more kinds of trim (rickrack, yarn, lace, ribbon, decorative buttons, braid, etc.) for students to add to their quilt squares.

3. Students may choose to write their names in a decorative fashion (use a variety of colors, write letters with dots, write block letters, etc.).

4. Take instant photographs of students to attach to quilt squares.

- -

FINAL FOCUS

Stewardship Notes

Materials: Bible with bookmark at 2 Corinthians 9:7, class notebook, pen.

Procedure: What are some of the things we learned today about giving and the different types of treasures?
Ask a volunteer to record students' responses in the class notebook. After students have given answers, volunteer reads aloud from the class notebook a few of the points from the previous lessons to help students remember what they have learned. **How is giving to God a way to be a good steward?**

Read 1 Corinthians 9:7 aloud. **What does this verse tell us about what we should give? What attitude should we have?**

Turning to the prayer journal section of the class notebook, volunteer makes note of prayer requests and answers that students have. To close, pray for the requests given, and then give volunteers an opportunity to say short prayers aloud. Invite students to thank God for the treasures He's given them and to ask God to show them ways to give their gifts to God.

44

© 2000 Gospel Light. Permission to photocopy granted. *The Great Stewardship Adventure for Kids*

THE LIVING IT! PAGE

KEY VERSE

"Each one should give what he has decided in his heart to give, not reluctantly or under compulsion, for God loves a cheerful giver."

2 Corinthians 9:7

The Challenge

Daniel 2:20

Ahoy there, mateys! Solve this puzzle and our pirate friend won't make you walk the plank. Use the letter and number under each line to find the coordinate on the map. When you've found each coordinate, unscramble the letters in the square to make a word. Do all 16 to uncover one of God's treasures just for you!

NEXT WEEK: TIME! Do you have it? How do you use it?

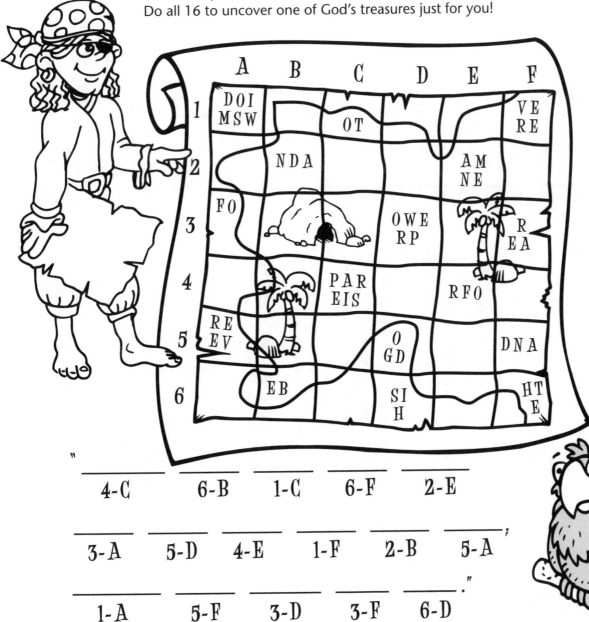

"
___ ___ ___ ___ ___
4-C   6-B   1-C   6-F   2-E

___ ___ ___ ___ ___ ___
3-A   5-D   4-E   1-F   2-B   5-A ;

___ ___ ___ ___ ___ ."
1-A   5-F   3-D   3-F   6-D

© 2000 Gospel Light. Permission to photocopy granted. *The Great Stewardship Adventure for Kids*

45

Daily Nuggets

Read these verses about attitudes that go a long way when we give.

DAY 1
Deuteronomy 15:7,8
What kinds of attitudes are we to have (or not have!) when we give?

DAY 2
Unscramble the letters or look up **Deuteronomy 15:4** to find out why we can give to others generously and with cheerful attitudes. (ANSWER: Because God has **ginve ssbingles** to us!) What good things has God given you?

DAY 3
Read **2 Corinthians 8:1-4** to find out about a church known for its generosity. Did they have a lot of money? What was their attitude toward giving?

DAY 4
Matthew 6:2-4
How does Jesus describe what hypocrites do when they give to the needy? What are we to do instead? What will be the result?

DAY 5
John 13:34,35
What command has God *given* us? What are we *giving* to God when we love others and follow His commands? **Bonus:** Get a detailed description of a loving attitude in **1 Corinthians 13:4-7**.

Topic for Conversation with God

Dear God, please show me the treasures you've given me that I can share with others.

Treasure in the Dark

Do you worry that you don't have as many treasures to share as others do? Read about this young girl who learned to share what she had and not think about what she didn't have.

When little Fanny (short for Frances) Crosby was only six weeks old, her eyes became infected. The doctor's treatment cured her infection—but it left her completely blind. She grew up feeling helpless and left out. What could she possibly do; what could she give? She couldn't see! Fanny was later taken to eye specialists, but they found her blindness could not be cured. Fanny was deeply disappointed. But she asked God if there was some work she could do. God answered her question then and there, she later recalled. What treasure did He show a blind girl she could share? Poetry!

Throughout her life, Fanny wrote over 5,000 poems. Sharing her poetry not only gave joy to those who read and sang her words, but also gave her great opportunities. She personally knew every president of the United States who held office during her lifetime, and she knew many other famous people. Many of her poems were set to music and are still sung today, years after her lifetime.

Fanny had asked God for treasure. She had shared the treasure she was given. And her words became a great treasure to many people!

This is the very first poem Frances Crosby wrote:

Oh, what a happy child I am,
Although I cannot see!
I am resolved that in this world
Contented I will be.

How many blessings I enjoy
That other people don't!
So weep or sigh because I'm blind?
I cannot, nor I won't!

© 2000 Gospel Light. Permission to photocopy granted. *The Great Stewardship Adventure for Kids*

Time Is of the Essence

LIFE FOCUS

God wants us to use our time wisely and get to know Him.

① GETTING PREPARED

AIMS

EXPLORE what we do with our time on a daily basis;
DISCUSS the best ways to be good stewards of our time;
DEVELOP a plan for spending time with God every day.

SCRIPTURE

Luke 10:38-42

KEY VERSE

"Be very careful, then, how you live—
not as unwise but as wise, making the most of every opportunity." Ephesians 5:15,16

Teacher's Devotional

In the well-known story of Mary and Martha, most of us may identify with Martha more often than with Mary. We know that on one level we should respond to Jesus in the way Mary did, yet we find ourselves, like Martha, worried, distracted and unable to sit quietly. Even spiritually mature adults know quite well that it's very easy to spend time in ways that crowd out our time with God.

   Throughout Scripture, we are instructed to do in a diligent way the work our maker has given us. But in the midst of our hard (and sometimes self-satisfied or anxious) work, we are asked by this story to consider what is actually needed. Do we need more and better programs, more efficient planning, even better-run prayer meetings? Or is that which is most needed simply time with Jesus,

© 2000 Gospel Light. Permission to photocopy granted. *The Great Stewardship Adventure for Kids*

listening to Him, "sitting at His feet"? Perhaps this story teaches us that it is better to sit figuratively at Jesus' feet and let Him reach and restore our hearts with His truth than it is to strive to serve Him in more and better ways.

Jesus said that only one thing is needed. Because He provides all we need—the talent, ability, gifts and skill to do the work He gives us—doesn't it make sense to sit at His feet regularly? We can trust Him to provide wisdom for managing our time, even while we stop our programs and lay aside our service and simply be with Him. As it's been said, "Good is the enemy of the best." May we take time, even from doing good, to spend time doing what is best, trusting God to help us manage the rest to His glory.

GETTING STARTED

What Do You Do?

Materials: None.

Procedure: Gather students together in the center of the room. As you ask the following question, point to a different corner or area of the room for each answer: **What do you usually do when you get home from school: play sports, do your homework, watch TV or play with a friend?** Students answer by moving to the designated areas, or they remain in the middle if none of the answers are true for them. Repeat activity with the following questions and answers: **What do you like to do on Saturday mornings: do chores, watch cartoons, go on family outings or play with friends? What do you like to do on school holidays: take a trip, read books at home, watch videos or play with friends?** Vary questions and answers according to your knowledge of your students and your class size. (If you have a small class, give fewer answers.) As time permits, invite volunteers to ask new questions and suggest answers about how students spend their time. Discuss activity: **How do you know if a person really likes to play basketball? How does that person spend his or her time? How can you tell if a person likes to draw?** Volunteers tell ideas. **Today we are going to talk about what good stewards do one of their most important treasures—time.**

GETTING INTO GOD'S WORD

Materials: Bibles.

Bible Study

Students open their Bibles to Luke 10. As you lead the following study, help students to discover answers in their Bibles.

What kinds of things does your family do to prepare for a very important visitor? How do grownups act when they don't think they are ready for an important visitor?

Mary and Martha were sisters who lived in Bethany with their brother Lazarus. They were friends of Jesus and they loved to have Him visit their home. One day, Jesus was coming to visit them and there were many things to do to get ready—many of the same things your family does. There were

© 2000 Gospel Light. Permission to photocopy granted. *The Great Stewardship Adventure for Kids*

bowls and plates and cups to wash. There were floors to be scrubbed, meat to be roasted, vegetables to be picked from the garden, and so on.

"Hurry, Mary!" Martha might have said. "I've swept the floor, but everything needs dusting. And where are the spices for the fish?"

Mary and Martha must have made sure the house was spotless. But there was still work left to do. They probably had to fetch the water, bake the bread and wash the grapes! They hustled and bustled and hurried all over the house to finish the work before Jesus arrived.

Soon a little cloud of dust rose over the horizon. Jesus and His friends were walking down the road. Mary probably shouted, "Jesus is here! He's here!" and ran out to greet Him while Martha stayed in the house. Martha could probably see a million things that still needed to be done!

As Jesus and the other guests came in, Martha continued to hurry around, making sure that everyone's feet were washed and that everyone was comfortable. She ran back and forth with bowls of water and plates of grapes and olives.

Suddenly Martha stopped and looked around. *Where is Mary?* she wondered. *Why isn't she helping me with all this work?* **Read Luke 10:39 to find out what Mary was doing.**

In Bible times, women usually did not sit in the room where a group of men sat. Women usually came in and out with food and drink for the men, perhaps listening while they worked. But on this day, Mary sat right at Jesus' feet and listened to everything He said. It was so wonderful just to be near Jesus! She had forgotten EVERYTHING else but listening to Him!

How do you think Martha felt when she saw Mary sitting by Jesus? Martha grumbled to herself as she finished getting dinner ready. Finally, Martha couldn't stand it any longer. **Read what she said to Jesus in Luke 10:40.** She was thinking so much about the work and the fact that Mary wasn't helping that she couldn't enjoy being with Jesus—even though HE was the reason she was working so hard to make everything wonderful.

Let's read in Luke 10:41 what Jesus said to Martha. Jesus understood how Martha felt. It seemed unfair to have to do all the work while Mary just sat and listened to Jesus. **What did Jesus tell Martha in verse 42?**

Martha had hurried and worked hard to help make Jesus and the other guests comfortable. She was doing a very GOOD thing. The only problem was that Martha had forgotten the BEST thing: Jesus had come to spend time with her and her family! That's why Jesus said Mary had chosen the better thing: spending time getting to know Jesus. That was something she would always remember. When the food was gone and the guests had left, Mary would still have the joy and wisdom she had gotten from spending time with Jesus!

Conclusion

Sometimes we're so busy doing lots of good things that we forget about doing the BEST things—things that help us to know Jesus better and things that show our love for Jesus. Being a good steward of God's gifts includes managing our time well. All the hours in a day are a gift from God for us to use wisely, and a part of using time wisely is taking time to know Him even MORE. Reading God's Word, praying to Him and talking with others about God are all ways we can spend our time each day getting to know Him better.

© 2000 Gospel Light. Permission to photocopy granted. *The Great Stewardship Adventure for Kids*

②4 GETTING FOCUSED

Use these discussion questions as you lead students in one or more of the Getting Focused activities:

- **What did Mary do when Jesus was at their house?** (She sat at His feet and learned from the things He was saying.) **What did Martha do when Jesus was at their house? What did Jesus say about their actions?**

- **What do you think were some of the things Martha may have been busy doing? Were they bad things to do with her time?** (Martha was busy preparing the food and making things nice for the guests. These aren't bad things to do, but a better thing would have been to learn from Jesus as Mary was doing.)

- **How were Mary and Martha the same? How were they different?**

- **What could everyone see about Mary from her actions? What do you learn about Martha from her actions?**

- **What are some of the things people know about you from your actions and the way you spend your time? What do others think is important to you?**

- **For Mary, a good thing kept her from doing the best thing. What are some times a good thing might keep a kid your age from the best thing?**

- **What are some ways you can spend time with Jesus? What is something you can do every day? What time will you set aside to do it?**

ACTIVE FOCUS:
Walk and Talk

Materials: Bible with bookmark at Ephesians 5:15,16; discussion questions; construction paper; markers; masking tape; music cassette/CD and player; large sheet of paper.

Preparation: Print the words "morning," "afternoon" and "evening" on separate sheets of construction paper. Lightly tape these papers (words facedown) along with blank papers to form a large circle on the floor, one paper for each student.

Procedure:

1. Each student stands on one of the papers. As you play a song from the cassette/CD, students walk around the circle, like a cakewalk. After several seconds, stop the music.

2. Each student picks up the paper on which he or she is standing. Students whose papers name times of day tell ways to get to know God at those times of day, or answer one of the discussion questions. To help students think of responses, ask one or more of the following questions: **What might you do in the morning to remind yourself of what God's Word says? What**

© 2000 Gospel Light. Permission to photocopy granted. *The Great Stewardship Adventure for Kids*

might you talk to God about in the afternoon? How could you take time in the evening to learn more about God? As students answer, print a brief description of their answers on large sheet of paper and post it on the wall. Repeat the activity as time permits, mixing up the papers with each round of the cakewalk.

3. After several rounds, give each student one of the papers used in the game, substituting time-of-day papers with blank sheets. Ask a student to read Ephesians 5:15,16 aloud. Referring to the list of answers, say, **These are all ways of doing what Ephesians 5:15,16 talks about.** Ask each student to choose one of the listed ways to be his or her plan for spending time with God every day. Students write their plan on their papers. Suggest students illustrate the words or draw designs around them. Students take home papers as reminders of their plan to spend time with God every day.

Table Alternative

If classroom space is limited, students pass papers around table while the music plays.

Discipline Tip

Never hesitate to join in a game with your students. They love to see you involved, and you can model proper responses and behavior for them. As you complete this activity along with students, briefly tell about a way you enjoy spending time with God at a particular time of day.

ART FOCUS: Play-Dough Plans

Materials: Bible with bookmark at Ephesians 5:15,16; discussion questions; ingredients and utensils for the recipe you choose; paper plates; large sheet of paper; marker.

Preparation: Make clay or dough, following one of these recipes. Each recipe makes enough for six to eight students.

Salt Dough: Mix 1 cup flour, 1 cup salt and 1 rounded teaspoon powdered alum in a bowl. Slowly add ½ cup water and knead until claylike.

Cornstarch Dough: Mix 2 cups cornstarch and 4 cups baking soda in pot. Add 2½ cups water. Cook and stir over medium heat for about 5 minutes until mixture thickens and resembles mashed potatoes. Remove from heat. Cover pot with a wet paper towel and allow dough to cool. Working on a surface covered with wax paper, kneed cooled dough for about 5 minutes.

Soapy Clay: Use a hand mixer to blend 4½ cups soap powder (such as Ivory Snow) with 6 tablespoons warm water in a bowl until mixture is the consistency of clay.

Procedure:

1. Give approximately ¼ cup of clay or dough on a paper plate to each student. Allow students time to experiment with clay or dough while you form the letters of a word that describes a way you get to know God. For example, form the word "Bible" to show that you enjoy reading and thinking about God's Word, the word "pray" to show that you like talking to God or the word "sing" to show that you like to sing songs about God.

2. Call students' attention to the word you formed and briefly describe why you enjoy getting to

© 2000 Gospel Light. Permission to photocopy granted. *The Great Stewardship Adventure for Kids*

know God in this way. **What other words could you make to show ways of getting to know God?** As students suggest ideas, print their responses on large sheet of paper. **These are all ways of doing what Ephesians 5:15,16 talks about.** Ask a volunteer to read Ephesians 5:15,16 aloud. **In our story today, who obeyed this verse? How?**

3. Each student chooses a word to make, referring to the ideas on the paper. After students complete their words, they leave them on paper plates to dry. Students take home words to display as reminders of ways to spend time with God every day.

Teaching Tips

1. Have students wash their hands after completing their sculptures. If a sink is unavailable, provide disposable wipes for students to use in cleaning their hands.

2. Take time to notice students' positive actions and comment on them. **Thank you for the way you are working on your sculptures.** Give extra help to students who need it. Your actions will help model God's love for them.

- -

FINAL FOCUS

Stewardship Notes

Materials: Bible with bookmark at Ephesians 5:15,16; class notebook; pen.

Procedure: What did we learn today about how we use the time God has given us? Ask a volunteer to record students' responses in the class notebook and read a few notes made during previous sessions to help students review what they have learned, reading ideas from today's session last. **We know that spending time with God and getting to know Him better is important for each member of His family.** Talk with interested students about becoming a member of God's family (see "Leading a Student to Christ" on p. 111).

Take a few moments to recite with students today's key verse, Ephesians 5:15,16. **What does this verse tell us to be careful about? What are some ways to "mak[e] the most of every opportunity"?**

Turning to the prayer journal section of the class notebook, ask volunteer to make note of prayer requests and answers that students have. Ask volunteers to share the reminders they made of their plans to spend time with God this week. **Let's take a few minutes to silently thank God for His love and that He gives us time that we can use well. Let's also ask God to help us remember to spend time with Him every day.** Close prayer by praying for the prayer requests and thanking God for the answers that have been given.

 © 2000 Gospel Light. Permission to photocopy granted. *The Great Stewardship Adventure for Kids*

THE LIVING IT! PAGE

SESSION 6

Topic for Conversation with God
Dear God, thank You that I can spend time with You every day. Help me to remember to _____ so that I can get to know You better.

The Challenge

NEXT WEEK: GIFTS! Which ones do you have?

Psalm 77:12
Break the code using the kids' code books to reveal the Bible verse.

For example:

B O Y

For example:

G I R L

(Plan to do this!)

© 2000 Gospel Light. Permission to photocopy granted. *The Great Stewardship Adventure for Kids*

KEY VERSE

"Be very careful, then, how you live—not as unwise but as wise, making the most of every opportunity." Ephesians 5:15,16

Daily Nuggets

God wants us to spend time getting to know Him, and we can find out the best ways to do that by reading His Word. Check out these verses about ways to know God better.

Day 1: Matthew 6:5-8
How does Jesus describe the right way to pray? What does God already know?

Day 2: Psalm 37:3-6
According to these verses, what can we do to be close to the Lord? When we do these things, what will God do?

Day 3: Psalm 119:10,11
What does the psalmist seek? What reason does the psalmist give for studying God's Word?

Day 4: Psalm 146:2
What two things does the psalmist plan to do as long as he lives? What are some reasons you might do these things?

Day 5: James 1:22-25
In addition to reading God's Word, what are we supposed to do? What will happen to anyone who does this?

Family Builder

As a family, list as many ways to spend time with God as you can within a designated amount of time. Choose a person to keep time, and a recorder to help you stay on track. You may want to continue playing with different categories (things to thank God for, ice cream flavors, character traits of Jesus, foreign countries, sports equipment, etc.).

Discovery and Exploration

There are 168 hours in a week. In a week, how many of those hours do you think you spend watching TV? playing with your dog? being in school? eating? Choose any of your favorite activities and guess how much time you spend on them in a week. This week add up the amount of time you spend doing those things. Is it more or less time than you thought? What surprises you most?

Too Much on My Plate

The wedding was over. Andy stood in line with his mother and father. *I can hardly believe my eyes!* Andy thought. Tables loaded with food stretched as far as he could see. Trays of sliced fruit, platters of cheeses, bowls of vegetables and dip—Andy helped himself! Then he added slices of turkey and ham to his plate.

"Shrimp?" asked the lady behind the serving table. He wasn't crazy about shrimp, but he nodded. THEN he saw the salads! Macaroni salad, spinach salad, cherry gelatin with whipped cream—they all went onto his plate. *This is great,* Andy smiled to himself. *My plate's piled!*

But as Andy followed his folks to sit down, he looked to his left. There sat a cart loaded with the most delicious-looking PIZZA he had EVER seen—pepperoni, ham and pineapple, EVERY kind of pizza! And not only was pizza Andy's very FAVORITE kind of pizza! And also a sign on the cart said THIS pizza was made by Santino's, his FAVORITE pizza place! Andy looked down at his plate. There was NO ROOM for PIZZA! Shoot, he thought. PIZZA! *If I'd only known. If I'd only looked ahead!* He was so disappointed, he almost had tears in his eyes!

As Andy sat looking at his plate, he heard his mother say, "There's already so much on my plate, I don't think I could." Andy glanced at his mother's plate. There was hardly ANY food on it! *Why did she say she had so much on her plate?* Andy wondered.

His mom looked over at his plate and said, "Sorry you missed the pizza. I'm sure you'd rather have eaten that than anything! Life can sure be like that—crammed so full of good stuff that there's no room for what's best. Did you see my friend who just left? She wanted me to go running with her early in the mornings. That's a GOOD thing, but it would take up time I have set aside to spend with God—and that's the BEST thing." Mom tapped the edge of Andy's plate. "So many GOOD things. And so little time. That's why it's important to make room for the BEST!"

© 2000 Gospel Light. Permission to photocopy granted. *The Great Stewardship Adventure for Kids*

Talents and More

LIFE FOCUS

God wants me to use the talents He's given me to serve Him and others.

1 GETTING PREPARED

AIMS

DISCOVER some talents kids have;
RECOGNIZE that God wants us to use our talents to serve Him and others;
DISCUSS how we can use our talents to serve God.

SCRIPTURE

Exodus 35:4—36:7; 40

KEY VERSE

"Each one should use whatever gift he has received to serve others." 1 Peter 4:10

Teacher's Devotional

Building the tabernacle was a tremendous effort of love and labor. When Moses gave the Lord's decrees about building the tabernacle, there was no foot-dragging! The Israelites brought the requested items willingly; those skilled in the needed crafts made themselves available and dependably did their finest work, teaching others those skills in the process. The entire community participated and there was more than was needed to do all the work. As a result, the place where God's people could come to worship Him freely became a joyful reality!

When we consider this ancient story, we see that availability to be used and dependability to complete the job and please God are perhaps the greatest talents a person can have. We don't need to feel pressured about whether or not our talents and abilities are of showcase quality. When we make ourselves available to God to do what He asks and are then dependable to complete what He gives us to do, we, like the Israelites, find that there is an even more beautiful result in a greater purpose. Encourage your students today to consider their unique gifts and abilities, but help them know that availability and dependability are two of the greatest!

© 2000 Gospel Light. Permission to photocopy granted. *The Great Stewardship Adventure for Kids*

② GETTING STARTED

What Gift?

Materials: Marker, small adhesive labels.

Preparation: On separate labels print these talents or positions: play soccer, care for younger children, read, do math, work with tools, science, make friends, cook, clean, sing, ride bike, skateboard, etc. Make one label for each student, repeating labels as needed.

Procedure: Place a label on a volunteer's back without letting him or her see what the label says. **The word on the label is a talent God may help you have.** Students (except volunteer) silently read the label and give clues to help volunteer guess what his or her label says. (A clue for the label "class president" might be "It is something you are elected to do. It has to do with school.") Continue giving clues until volunteer guesses the label. Volunteer then chooses another label to put on another student's back. Students continue giving clues and guessing as time permits. **What are some other talents God has given kids your age? What do you enjoy doing?** Volunteers answer. **During our class today, be thinking about the talents God has given you.**

③ GETTING INTO GOD'S WORD

Materials: Bibles.

Bible Study

Students find Exodus 35 in their Bibles. As you lead the following study, assist students to discover answers in their Bibles.

What do you think every church building needs? Why? Students respond. **What would you add to or take away from our church building? Today we're going to discover how God's people used their talents, gifts and abilities to complete the very first building set aside for people to use to worship God.**

Moses and the Israelites were traveling through the desert on their way to the new land God had promised them. God helped the Israelites while they traveled by giving them pillars of cloud and fire to guide them as well as food and water. But there was one thing the Israelites did not have—a place to worship God. In Egypt, they'd had no special place where people gathered to worship the Lord. And in the desert, they were traveling all the time. They certainly weren't going to build a building and then move on! God had a plan to solve that problem.

God told Moses all about it. The people were to build a huge tent that God called a Tabernacle. It was to remind them that the Lord lived among them. It would be a place where the people could get together and worship Him. The people would be able to take this Tabernacle apart and carry it with them as they moved from place to place on their way to the land that God had promised them.

Now, you might think a tent wouldn't be a very pretty place. But THIS tent would be the most beautiful tent the people had ever seen! **Let's read Exodus 35:5-9 to find why the Tabernacle would be so beautiful. What did Moses tell the people to bring? Which item would you**

© 2000 Gospel Light. Permission to photocopy granted. *The Great Stewardship Adventure for Kids*

like to have brought as an offering if you had been there?

"What's more," Moses continued, "anyone who has a special skill and who is willing, can help MAKE the Tabernacle!"

That very day people began bringing jewelry and brightly colored yarns and oil and cloth and wood—all the things Moses had asked for. Every single gift was given eagerly and willingly because the people knew that each gift was an offering to the Lord and would help them have a special place to worship Him.

Read Exodus 35:31,32. Where did the skill for doing craftwork come from? Read Exodus 35:34,35 to learn about other talents given by God. Soon the Israelites' camp was as busy as a beehive! Some people melted down jewelry for the gold. Some cut boards, and some covered the boards with gold. Some people spun bright thread, some made cloth from the goats' hair, and some dyed the ram skins red.

Other people worked to make the special furniture to go inside the Tabernacle. There was a beautiful lampstand, a table, the altar for burning incense and a beautiful box called the Ark of the Covenant. The Ark of the Covenant was a special wooden chest that was covered with gold and had beautiful golden angels on top of it. The Ark held the stone tablets with the Ten Commandments written on them.

Still other people made a big bronze basin (or bowl) for washing and a bronze altar for sacrifices. People who weren't working on these projects were busy making robes for the priests or one of the hundreds of other jobs!

Each morning the Israelites brought more gifts to give to the Lord. **How much do you think the people brought? Let's read Exodus 36:6,7 to find out.** The people brought so much, Moses had to tell them to stop!

Day after day the people worked and worked and WORKED until, finally, someone put the last stitch of blue thread in the fine linen curtains, and the last piece of bright golden furniture looked just right. The people had finished their work—and they had followed the Lord's instructions EXACTLY. They had used their wealth, their skills and their time to make something wonderful that would please God. Then Moses inspected everything they had made.

"You've done a good job!" Moses told the people. "On the first day of the first month, we'll set it all up!"

The people could hardly wait for the big day to arrive. When it finally came, Moses followed the Lord's instructions step-by-step and put together the most beautiful tent any of them had ever seen.

FIRST—the base, the frames, the posts and all the outer coverings were set up. Then the Ark of the Covenant was placed in a special room called the Most Holy Place. Only the high priest would be permitted behind the curtain that separated this room, and he could enter there only once a year! The Most Holy Place was special because it was where the Lord would meet and talk with the high priest and forgive the Israelites' sins.

NEXT—the golden table, lampstand and altar of incense were set up in a second room called the holy place. Only the priests would be permitted in the holy place.

What was placed in the courtyard around the Tabernacle? Read about the items in Exodus 40:29,30. Moses presented special offerings to the Lord, just as God commanded him. The priests washed their hands and feet in the bronze bowl whenever they entered the Tabernacle.

The Israelites would come to the Tabernacle courtyard to worship the Lord. They would bring sacrifices (animals that had been killed in payment for the people's sins) and offer them to the Lord at the altar. Giving sacrifices was the way the Israelites told the Lord they were sorry for their sins. When they did this, the Lord forgave their sins.

FINALLY—the curtains were put up around the courtyard. Now God's special tent stood complete. It was beautiful. **What do you think happened next? Let's read Exodus 40:34 to find out.** Moses and the people knew God was with them. Now the people had a special place where they could come together to worship God!

Conclusion

The Israelites used their goods, their talents and skills, and their time to build a very special place in which they could praise God together. And today, we can still use our talents, abilities, gifts and skills to do things that please God, just as the Israelites pleased God by obeying Him and making the Tabernacle.

4 GETTING FOCUSED

Use these discussion questions as you lead students in one or more of the Getting Focused activities:
- **What did the Israelites give to help the building of the Tabernacle?**
- **Where did the skills and talents come from that the Israelites used to build the Tabernacle?**
- **Why do you think the Israelites were so willing to help build the Tabernacle?**
- **What part of the Tabernacle would you have wanted to make? Why? What skills do you have that you might have used if you had been there?**
- **What are some times when people you know have donated money or fine things to pay for a big project that is for everyone?**
- **What are some things a kid your age can do to show love for God? What ways can you use your skills and talents to please God at home? at school? at church?**

ACTIVE FOCUS: Specially Gifted

Materials: Bible with bookmark at 1 Peter 4:10, discussion questions, large sheet of paper, markers, index cards, colored envelopes, ribbons, scissors.

Preparation: Print the words of 1 Peter 4:10 on large sheet of paper.

Procedure:

1. Ask a volunteer to read 1 Peter 4:10 aloud. **God has given us many gifts. He's given us people who love us and good food to eat. He's also given each of us special abilities and talents. We may not know what our talents are right now, but we can be certain that each one of us has a least one special ability.**

2. **What are some abilities that you have? What do you enjoy doing?** Volunteers respond. Distribute an index card to each student. On index cards, students print a talent

 © 2000 Gospel Light. Permission to photocopy granted. *The Great Stewardship Adventure for Kids*

or ability (swimming, singing, good at math, patience, gardening, fast runner, etc.) and then place their cards in envelopes and seal. Students tie ribbon around envelopes to represent gifts. As students work, ask the discussion questions.

3. Collect envelopes from students who then form a large circle. Hand one envelope to a student. Referring to the verse on the large sheet of paper as needed, students say one word of the verse as they pass the envelope around the circle. The student who says the last word of the verse opens the envelope and reads the gift written on the card. **How could someone use the talent of (swimming well) to help someone else?** (Teach someone to swim. Be a good sport.) **By using the gifts God has given to us in ways that help others, we are giving our love and thanks to God!** Starting with the next student in the circle, repeat the verse in the same manner. Game continues until each student has opened an envelope.

Teaching Tip

Vary the way students pass the envelope for each round: pass envelope through their legs, skip a person or two, pass envelope behind their backs, hold envelopes under their chins to pass envelopes, etc. Ask students to suggest interesting ways to pass the envelopes.

Age-Level Tip

Fourth, fifth and sixth graders are moving from reliance on adult approval to greater desire for peer approval. This is a normal part of the maturation process that will eventually help them to become healthy adults. But what can you do as their teacher to keep them open and able to communicate with you?

One way to keep communication flowing is to listen more than you talk. Your students are not mentally or physically ready for a great deal of direct instruction (teaching by lecturing). Learning that involves their minds and their bodies is most likely to reach their hearts.

ART FOCUS: Gift Box

Materials: Bible with bookmark at 1 Peter 4:10, discussion questions, white butcher paper or wrapping paper, one shoe box or gift box for each student, tape, scissors, glue, art materials (die-cut shapes, magazines, ribbon or rickrack, glue, glitter, stickers, rubber stamps and ink pad, etc.).

Preparation: Make a sample gift box following the directions below.

Procedure:

1. **What are some of the talents or abilities God has given to you?** Volunteers respond. Read, or ask a volunteer to read, 1 Peter 4:10 aloud. **What does this verse tell us we should do with the gifts we have been given?** (Serve others.) **By using our talents or abilities to serve others, we are showing how thankful we are for the gifts God gives us. It's like we are giving the gifts back to God to show our love for Him. Let's cover a box with the gifts God has given us and discuss ways we can use our talents to serve God and others.**

2. Display sample you made. **This box shows some of the talents and abilities God has given me. What are some ways I could use them to help others?** Volunteers respond.

3. Students cover boxes with butcher paper or wrapping paper. Then students use art materials to decorate boxes with pictures of the gifts they have been given (magazine pictures of people playing sports, math equations, pictures of people singing, etc.). As students work, ask volunteers to

tell about the gifts that God has given them. Lead students in discussing different ways these gifts can be given back to God by helping others. Ask discussion questions to extend the conversation.

Teaching Tips

1. Providing a variety of unique materials for students to use will increase student interest in the project.

2. Learning activities involving creative art experiences provide an enjoyable and effective way for students to express what they have learned and to plan ways to put that learning into action. As you use art activities, remember that the learning *process* is more important than the end *product*. As you select and use art experiences, focus the student's attention on the Bible truth concerned, not on the result or quality of the work.

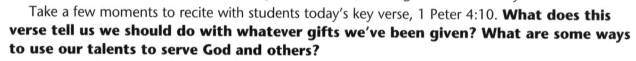

FINAL FOCUS

Stewardship Notes

Materials: Bible with bookmark at 1 Peter 4:10, class notebook, pen.

Procedure: What are some of the different talents or abilities we talked about today? Where do these gifts come from? Ask a volunteer to record students' ideas and comments in the class notebook. Read a few notes made during previous sessions to help students review what they have learned, reading ideas from today's session last.

Take a few moments to recite with students today's key verse, 1 Peter 4:10. **What does this verse tell us we should do with whatever gifts we've been given? What are some ways to use our talents to serve God and others?**

Turning to the prayer journal section of the class notebook, volunteer makes note of prayer requests and answers that students have. Ask volunteers to tell a gift from the lists they made and ways they can use the gift to serve God. **Let's take a few minutes to thank God for giving us our talents and other gifts.** Students pray short prayers thanking God for the talents He has given to other members of the class and for prayer requests. Close by asking for God's help to use our gifts to serve Him and others.

© 2000 Gospel Light. Permission to photocopy granted. *The Great Stewardship Adventure for Kids*

THE LIVING IT! PAGE

SESSION 7

KEY VERSE

"Each one should use whatever gift he has received to serve others."
1 Peter 4:10

NEXT WEEK: MONEY! What can you do with it?

1 Peter 4:10
"Each one should use whatever gift he has received to serve others."

START

FINISH

gift
he
received
gift
others
Each
whatever
whatever
to
serve
should
has
should
use
to
one
serve
received
others
use

The Challenge → Go through the maze, passing the words of the Bible verse in order to find the correct path.

© 2000 Gospel Light. Permission to photocopy granted. *The Great Stewardship Adventure for Kids*

Discovery and Exploration

Make a list of things you enjoy doing. What ways could God use these things?

Family Builder

Have a family talent night! Take photographs or video-tape each family member using his or her talent or working on a hobby.

Daily Nuggets

You've been given gifts and talents.
But these verses reveal other incredible gifts from God!

DAY 1: John 14:15-18
What did Jesus promise us? Who'd He send to keep us company forever? When is a time it would help a kid your age to remember this?

DAY 2: John 14:27
When are some times your heart might "be troubled"? What does that mean? What does Jesus give us so that we don't need to feel that way?

DAY 3: 2 Timothy 1:7
What has God's given you? What are some things you can do, knowing God has given this to us?

DAY 4: 1 Corinthians 1:7-9
Who's going to be faithful? What do these verses promise from God? When is a time it might be good to remember these verses?

DAY 5: Hebrews 4:16
How should we feel when we ask God for help? What has God done so that we can feel this way?

Great Gifts

The baby was so sickly and frail, the men who had stolen him abandoned him in the woods. He wasn't worth keeping, they decided. (Were they ever wrong!) But the little boy lived. He was adopted by the Carver family and he grew, but he was not very strong. As George helped around the house of the folks who adopted him, the Carvers could see that though there were things George could not do, he could nurse the sickest plant back to health. George understood plants and animals in an unusual way. And George's gifted drawings seemed almost alive! Even so, there wasn't much expected in the way of a future for a newly freed slave child in the 1860s. The Carvers had no idea then that George's gifts and abilities would change the course of history!

When he was nine years old, George went to a school that was too far away for him to be able to walk to. The Carvers had no money to pay for a place for George to live in near the school; but in addition to using his gifts and talents, George had learned he could trust God. The experience he gained working around the Carver home had prepared him for jobs that kept him earning money for the whole time he was in school. Eventually, George graduated from college, and then he went on to study at Iowa State University where he got a master's degree in agriculture. George was such a gifted painter that he planned to go to Paris to study art. But God had bigger plans. He was going to use all of George's gifts!

In Alabama, another former slave, Booker T. Washington, had established a school especially for newly freed slaves. He believed that until African-Americans had better educations, they'd be stuck in slavelike jobs all their lives. Washington invited George to teach at his school, Tuskegee Institute. George accepted. For 47 years, he not only taught students but also painted and did research on plants—research that completely changed farming in the South! He traveled the world and spoke before Congress, but he always had time to teach his weekly Bible study and to "adopt" students who needed a friend. And how did George change things? He said God gave him ideas for new ways to use the humble peanut. If you've ever eaten peanut butter, it's because of George Washington Carver—artist, musician, scientist, teacher and great steward of God's many gifts.

© 2000 Gospel Light. Permission to photocopy granted. *The Great Stewardship Adventure for Kids*

Money Matters

LIFE FOCUS

Treasure God rather than money.

1 GETTING PREPARED

AIMS

EXPLORE the meaning of the word "tithe";
REALIZE what we do with our money can show our love for God;
PLAN ways to show that we treasure God more than money.

SCRIPTURE

Luke 12:13-34

KEY VERSE

"Store up for yourselves treasure in heaven, where moth
and rust do not destroy, and where thieves do not break in and steal.
For where your treasure is, there your heart will be also." Matthew 6:20,21

Teacher's Devotional

Just after Jesus told the parable of the rich fool, He said that "life is more than food, and the body more than clothes" (Luke 12:23). In a society where striving to get ahead, plan a secure retirement or have better benefits is not only common but also applauded, this story and statement should stop us in our tracks!

Jesus calls the man a fool who takes his surplus, the blessing of God, and hoards it for himself. That should cause us to ask ourselves, *To what purpose does God bless us? Why are we given more than the bare necessities?* As we take a hard look at common attitudes toward money and security in this lesson, we need to consider our focus as Christians. When we are intent on making things better for ourselves in this earthly life at the material and spiritual cost of others who need our help, is that a narrow way of thinking? Is it idolatry, the worship of Mammon, to gather earthly benefits the way the rich fool planned to gather his surplus into barns?

This passage requires us to deeply consider our call to be Christlike and to incorporate the way

© 2000 Gospel Light. Permission to photocopy granted. *The Great Stewardship Adventure for Kids*

we use our surplus as an essential element of Christian stewardship. Jesus promises that instead of a grasping, worried existence focused on material security, He wants us to invest in His kingdom, seek Him first and allow Him to add to our lives.

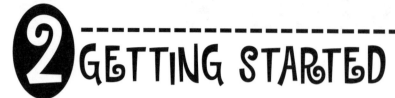

2 GETTING STARTED

Tithing Math

Materials: Paper towels, small resealable bags, stick pretzels.

Procedure: How many of you have heard the word "tithe" before? What do you think it means? Volunteers respond. **In Old Testament times, people were expected to give back to God one-tenth of everything they earned. This is called a tithe, or one-tenth.** Distribute a paper towel and a resealable bag to each student. Students hold bags open as you pour a random number of stick pretzels into the bags. Then students place pretzels on their paper towels and count them. **Tithing means giving back to God one-tenth of everything God gives you. How many pretzels would one-tenth of the pretzels you received be?** For every ten pretzels students count, one is placed back in the resealable bag to be given back and nine are kept out to be eaten during the Bible Study. **Today we'll learn about ways our use of money can show our love for God.**

3 GETTING INTO GOD'S WORD

Materials: Bibles.

Bible Study

Students find Luke 12:13-34 in their Bibles. As you lead the following study, help students to discover answers in their Bibles.

What would you do with lots of money? Students respond. **It's fun to think about what we would do with lots of money. Today we're going to hear a story Jesus told about a man who had plenty of money.**

Jesus had been talking to people about what is important in life when suddenly a man spoke up.

"Look, Jesus," he said, "will you tell my brother to split our father's inheritance with me?" In Bible times, a father's money and possessions were divided between his sons, but the oldest son received twice as much as the younger son. The Bible doesn't say whether the older brother wasn't giving this man any of the inheritance or if the man just wanted more than he was legally entitled to.

But Jesus knew the real reason behind this man's question. This man was asking for Jesus' help in the situation with his brother because money was the MOST important thing to this man. It was even more important than getting along with his brother! **Read what Jesus warned this man in Luke 12:15.**

And then Jesus told a story that is sometimes called the parable of the rich fool. **Let's find out why this rich man is called foolish.**

 © 2000 Gospel Light. Permission to photocopy granted. *The Great Stewardship Adventure for Kids*

Read the beginning of the parable in Luke 12:16,17. What different things could the man have done with his extra crops? The man could have left some of his crops in the fields for poor people to harvest. The man could have taken the extra grain to the market and sold it. He could have given his extra grain away. He could even have started a bakery!

What do you think the man decided to do? Compare your idea with what he did. Read Luke 12:18,19. What did the man decide to do? Why? The rich man probably thought he wouldn't have to work so hard next year—he would take some time off! Maybe he dreamed about all the stuff he could buy with the money from his crops—a new coat, more chickens, statues for his house, maybe even a bigger house! Keeping his crops for himself was all this man thought about. And THAT was his problem. He put all his hope for the future into building bigger barns so that he could KEEP his own stuff for HIMSELF.

Read Luke 12:20 to find out what happened next. The man didn't know it, but he was going to die that very night! The rich man had spent all his time thinking about how to keep the crops for himself so that he would have them later, and now there wasn't going to BE a "later"! He wasn't going to need those crops anymore. **How did God describe this man?** No wonder the man was called a fool! He'd paid attention to only one thing all his life and missed the most important thing: knowing and loving God.

At the end of the story, Jesus described what someone is like who is a fool. **Read verse 21 to discover what Jesus was telling the crowd. What do you think it means to be rich toward God?** A person who is rich toward God puts God first. A person rich toward God has been spending time getting to know God, loving and obeying Him.

When Jesus finished His story, He turned to His listening disciples and pointed to the birds in the sky. "Look at the ravens," He said. "They don't store their food in barns. But God takes care of them. And you are worth MUCH more than these birds, so DON'T WORRY about anything!"

He then pointed to some beautiful flowers on the hill. **Read Luke 12:27 to see what Jesus said about them**. Jesus went on to say, "If God takes care of lilies, he will certainly give you clothes, too. YOU are MORE important than these flowers!" **Read Luke 12:31 to find what Jesus said is most important.** Someone who seeks God's kingdom is a person who depends on God and loves and obeys Him. **Let's read Luke 12:34 together. What does it mean?** Jesus meant that what we do shows what's important to us. If God is our treasure, it will show in the way we live. If our possessions and money are our treasure, that will show as well!

Jesus' listeners must have thought carefully about their own worrying and focusing on getting more money. Imagine knowing that they could trust in God. His gifts of loving care are better than anything money can buy. And they last forever!

Conclusion

This parable makes it clear that money and possessions don't last and can't make us happy. What we do with our money shows what we think is really important and how we feel about God. What God gives us is much better than anything money can buy! His gifts—eternal life, a relationship with Him, peace and love—are the only things that can make us truly happy because these are the things we truly need! That's why Jesus wants us to treasure God and our relationship with Him more than anything else.

© 2000 Gospel Light. Permission to photocopy granted. *The Great Stewardship Adventure for Kids*

24 GETTING FOCUSED

Use these discussion questions as you lead students in one or more of the Getting Focused activities:

- **What kind of choices did the rich man make? What could he have done differently?**
- **What did the rich man's actions tell about his attitudes toward God? toward others?**
- **Why might someone think that money is the most important thing to have?**
- **What does it mean to be rich toward God?** (To treasure God more than money or possessions. To study and know His Word.) **What are some things a person can do to show he or she is rich toward God? What difference do you think these actions will make in a person's life?**
- **How does God care for birds and flowers? How is that like the ways He cares for us? How is it different?**
- **Why does Jesus say we should not worry about having stuff? What should we do instead? What are some ways a kid your age can seek God's kingdom?** (Pray to God. Read His Word. Talk with others about God.)
- **How can we use the money God gives us to show our love for Him?**
- **What are some reasons we give our money to God?** (To remind us He gave us everything we have. To show our thankfulness to Him. To help others.)

ACTIVE FOCUS:
Treasure Hunt

Materials: Bibles, discussion questions, index cards, marker, beanbag.

Preparation: On separate index cards, print the following fill-in-the-blank sentences:

"One thing kids might treasure or value more than God is _____."

"One thing that can happen to that treasure is _____."

"What I spend my money on when I'm at _____ shows _____."

"One way I can show that loving God is most important to me is by _____."

"I think that _____ is a way to store up treasure in heaven."

"To show that God is more important than money, I plan to _____."

Procedure:

1. Read, or ask a volunteer to read, Matthew 6:20,21. **According to this verse, why are we supposed to "store up . . . treasure in heaven"? What does the verse mean when it says "there your heart will be also"?** (We spend our time and attention on the things we treasure.) **Let's play a game to help us plan ways to show that we treasure God more than money.**

© 2000 Gospel Light. Permission to photocopy granted. *The Great Stewardship Adventure for Kids*

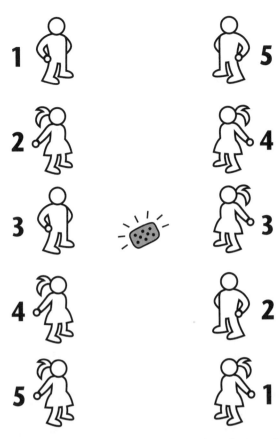

2. Divide class into two teams. Teams line up as in sketch. Place beanbag on the floor between the lines of students. Assign each student a number. Use the same set of numbers for each team. To begin play, call out any one of the numbers you have assigned children. Both of the students with this number quickly run to get the beanbag and return to their teams. The first student to get the beanbag and return to his or her team selects one of the index cards and completes the sentence starter or answers a discussion question. Return beanbag to playing area and continue game as time allows.

Teaching Tip

Play a few practice rounds. Students will learn the rules best by actually playing the game.

Learning Tip

Preteens (and the rest of us, too) are far more strongly influenced by examples they see than by words they hear. At an age when kids are looking beyond the family for role models, a caring, friendly teacher can be someone to emulate. However, you must be doing things students can emulate! If you want them to memorize Bible verses, memorize along with them. If you want them to study their Bibles, share with them weekly what you have learned from your personal Bible study. If you want students to become comfortable telling what Jesus means to them, tell them often what Jesus means to you. Frequently sharing God's work in your own life helps students see that your friendship with Jesus is real, fresh and worth imitating!

ART FOCUS:
Bank on It!

Materials: Bible with bookmark at Matthew 6:20,21; discussion questions; materials for bank of your choice.

Preparation: Make a sample bank following directions below.

Procedure:

1. **We can show our love for God by the things we do with our money.** Read, or ask a volunteer to read, Matthew 6:20,21. **According to this verse, where should we be storing up treasures?** (Heaven.) **How do we do that?** (By using our money, talents and time to accomplish things that will last forever.) **What will happen as a result?** (That's where our hearts will be.) **What does it mean to say our hearts are in heaven?** (That we treasure God instead of money.) **What are some things other people might notice us doing if we treasure God instead of money?** Volunteers

© 2000 Gospel Light. Permission to photocopy granted. *The Great Stewardship Adventure for Kids*

respond. **Today we are going to make banks to help us remember where our real treasure is.**

2. Lead students in making offering banks. Students take home finished offering banks to collect change, allowance or money they earn. Students may bring collected money to church at a designated time and give offering to a church project.

Can Bank: Give each student a clean can with plastic lid (potato chip, nuts, baking powder, etc.) in which you have cut a slit large enough to insert money. Students measure and cut sheets of construction paper to wrap around cans. Students draw on papers ways to offer love, time, abilities and money to God and then wrap papers around cans, securing with tape. Students may also tie ribbon around cans.

Box Bank: Give each student a small box (check box, small gift box, etc.) in which you have cut a slit large enough to insert money. Students cover boxes with wrapping paper and then use markers to write slogans about treasuring God.

3. As students work, ask discussion questions to extend conversation about planning ways to show that we treasure God more than money.

Learning Tip

What should you do if you ask a question and no one says anything? First, if you've asked a thought-provoking question, assume that students need at least a few moments to think. Be silent for three to five seconds and then repeat or rephrase the question. If you still get no response, acknowledge that it was a hard question, tell how you would answer it and move on. Be sure the questions you are asking are clear and open-ended, not too vague or intimidating.

FINAL FOCUS

Stewardship Notes

Materials: Bible with bookmark at 1 Peter 4:10, class notebook, pen.

Procedure: What did we learn today about how giving money can show our love for God? Ask a volunteer to record students' ideas and comments in the class notebook. Volunteer reads a few notes made during previous sessions to help students review what they have learned, reading ideas from today's session last.

Read Matthew 6:20,21 aloud. **What does this verse tell us could happen if you store up treasures here on earth? Where is the best place to store treasure? Besides giving money in a church offering, what are some other ways we can give money for God's work?**

Turning to the prayer journal section of the class notebook, volunteer makes note of prayer requests and answers that students have. If students did the art activity, ask volunteers to display the banks they made and describe how the banks will help them as they plan ways to give money to God. **Let's take a few minutes to think of a specific way we can give money to God this week.** Ask students to pray silently, asking for God's help to find ways to give money to Him. Give students time for silent prayer. Close prayer by thanking God for all the gifts He gives us: money, time, talents and the ability to use these gifts to show our love for Him.

© 2000 Gospel Light. Permission to photocopy granted. *The Great Stewardship Adventure for Kids*

THE Living IT! PAGE

SESSION 8

NEXT WEEK: HABITS! Do you have any?

KEY VERSE

"Store up for yourselves treasure in heaven, where moth and rust do not destroy, and where thieves do not break in and steal. For where your treasure is, there your heart will be also." Matthew 6:20,21

1 Chronicles 16:29

"Ascribe to the Lord the glory due his name. Bring an offering and come before him; worship the Lord."

Family Builder

Have a financial report! Find out about ways that your family uses money. How much goes for car repairs? vacations? How much do you give? save?

The Challenge

Follow the arrows to find the path that goes through all the words of the verse.

© 2000 Gospel Light. Permission to photocopy granted. *The Great Stewardship Adventure for Kids*

Topic for Conversation with God

Dear God, sometimes it's hard to show how important You are to me. Please help me . . .

Who's Rich?

OLD UNCLE HERBIE, HE WAS SO RICH... I KEPT HIS MONEY- BUT GAVE HIM THIS DITCH!
DON'T BE A FOOL LIKE ME. I WASTED ALL MY HOURS! NOW ALL I CAN DO IS PUSH UP THESE FLOWERS!!
I SPENT MY WHOLE LIFE AND SOUL MAKING MONEY. I IGNORED GOD AND HIS RICHES, THIS ISN'T FUNNY
SILVER+GOLD I HAD A LOT! NOW ALL I HAVE IS THIS SIX-FOOT PLOT!
SHE HAD EVERYTHING MONEY COULD BUY. NOW IT'S THE GRAVE WHERE SHE HAS TO LIE...LAY?
"EVERYBODY GOES SOMETIME..." THAT'S WHAT THEY SAY. I DIDN'T EXPECT IT TO HAPPEN TODAY!!

Daily Nuggets

Read these verses to find out what the Bible says about different kinds of treasures.

DAY 1 • Deuteronomy 6:10-13
What gifts from God are listed here? Choose one and describe how it could be used to help others.

DAY 2 • Psalm 19:7-11
What's more precious than gold? How can you show that God's Word is important to you?

DAY 3 • Proverbs 2:3-5
What is it we are to search for like hidden treasure? How can you search for that this week?

DAY 4 • 1 Timothy 6:18,19
What are we supposed to be rich in? What are we supposed to be willing to do? Name one way you could do that this week.

DAY 5 • Colossians 2:2,3
According to this verse, what is the key to the treasure? What could you do to gain wisdom this week?

Buried Treasure

Sara and Jenna had agreed that burying the money in their treasure jar was the best way to hide it. But their big brother had been teasing them about keeping their money in the jar and he might take their jar if he could find it! So the sisters took their treasure jar to the field across the road. They wandered around the field, just in case anyone was looking. They finally chose a spot, dug a hole and buried their savings. The girls dusted off their hands, smiling. Their brother would NEVER find their treasure jar!

A few months later, Sara had earned several more dollars. Waving the bills excitedly, she told Jenna, "Let's dig up the treasure jar!"

"You DO remember where we buried it, don't you, Sara?" Jenna asked. The girls looked at each other in disbelief. How could they have forgotten? But they HAD! They swallowed hard. Now they had NOTHING!

They went to their mother and chokingly told her what had happened. She held them both while they wiped their noses and brushed away tears. Then she said, "I can see that money jar was very important to both of you. It must have been fun to bury it like treasure. But I don't think there's anything you can do besides go out into the field and try to remember where you buried it. While you're out there, think of other kinds of treasure you ALREADY have!"

The girls were quiet as they walked to the field. They didn't have ANY treasure now! What did Mom mean, treasure they already had?

"Hm," Sara said. "I bet Mom means treasures that aren't money and stuff. Well, we have each other. We're sisters forever. And we have parents. Some kids don't."

"We have brothers, too. But THAT'S not treasure!" said Jenna as their little brother Rob came up.

"Whatcha doin'?" he asked.

"Looking for treasure!" said Sara.

"Oh. Like the jar you buried?" Rob asked.

"WHAT? Were you SPYING on us?!" growled Jenna.

Rob looked sheepish. "Well, I DID see where you buried your jar."

"Oh, ROB! Our HERO!" cried Sara. She hugged him. "WHERE?!"

It wasn't long before Sara and Jenna were on their knees, digging down in the spot Rob pointed out. YES! There was the treasure jar!

Sara looked at Jenna. "I guess Rob IS one of the treasures we have. And our treasure *person* helped us find our treasure *jar*!"

© 2000 Gospel Light. Permission to photocopy granted. *The Great Stewardship Adventure for Kids*

Total Fitness

LIFE FOCUS

Practicing good habits every day helps us be ready to serve God.

① GETTING PREPARED

AIMS

GRAPH actions kids do every day;
UNDERSTAND that good habits prepare us to serve God;
DISCUSS and choose good habits we can practice every day.

SCRIPTURE

Daniel 1; 5; 6

KEY VERSE

"Love the Lord your God with all your heart and with all your soul and with all your strength." Deuteronomy 6:5

Teacher's Devotional

Successful people are often interviewed and asked to outline their regular habits. They may cite promptly returning telephone calls, exercising regularly or making lists as habits that have contributed to their success. Martin Luther was a successful individual who accomplished astonishing things during his lifetime. His one regular habit? Because he was so busy and had so much to do every day, he declared that starting the day with three hours of prayer was absolutely necessary! He had learned the truth that beginning each day in fellowship with God sets the day in order and leads to remarkable accomplishments. He built this holy habit over the years and it showed in his life.

Perhaps Luther learned this habit from reading the book of Daniel. Daniel was well known in Babylon as a man who prayed three times a day, on his knees with his window open toward Jerusalem, every day, year after year. Regardless of changes in government or changes in weather, there he was. He made a habit of obeying his conscience regardless of any outside pressure. He made a habit of going to God for wisdom. What success did such habits of spiritual fitness give him? He was famous for his integrity and wisdom, an advisor under several kings and a man who

© 2000 Gospel Light. Permission to photocopy granted. *The Great Stewardship Adventure for Kids*

exhibited godliness in every situation. Angels saved his life in the lions' den!

Consider the habits you have made over time. Which habits bring you closer to God? Which make you the more fit to serve the King, more successful in His kingdom? Which habits can you recommend to your students? Even if we think our habits are hidden from others, the fruit of them shows in everything we do. Like Daniel, we need to faithfully practice godly habits that make us fit to love God with all our heart, soul and strength.

GETTING STARTED

Graphic Actions

Materials: Materials for graph(s) of your choice.

Procedure: Lead students to complete one or both of these graphs to show actions kids do every day.

Candy Graph: Students tell some things they do immediately after school. (Homework, eat a snack, play soccer, etc.) Print several different actions at the top of separate columns on a large sheet of paper. Each student places a piece of wrapped candy in the column representing what he or she does after school. Repeat with other times of the day (after dinner, when they first wake up, etc.).

Human Graph: Designate four different spots along a wall to be four actions that kids do immediately after school. Students line up to show what they do after school (longest line equals most popular action). Repeat with other actions at other times of the day.

What else do kids your age do every day? When people do the same thing every day, we say that they have a habit. Some habits are good, and some habits are bad. Today we'll be talking about good habits that can help us be good stewards.

GETTING INTO GOD'S WORD

Materials: Bibles.

Bible Study

Students open their Bibles to Daniel 1. As you lead the following study, help students to discover answers in their Bibles.

What is the first thing you do every morning? What do you do every night right before you go to sleep? Volunteers respond. **When people do the same thing every day at the same time, we say that they have a habit. Today in our Bible story we're going to hear about someone whose habits helped him become fit to serve God in the very best ways. Let's find out more about what happened.**

Daniel was a teenager who lived in Jerusalem about 600 years before Jesus was born. At that time, people from the country of Babylonia had taken over most of that part of the WORLD! Daniel and other people from Jerusalem were taken to Babylon (the capital city) as captives. Daniel and some of his friends were chosen to be trained as workers for the king of Babylon.

© 2000 Gospel Light. Permission to photocopy granted. *The Great Stewardship Adventure for Kids*

Daniel and his friends were given Babylonian names. They were given Babylonian food to eat that was supposed to make them strong. BUT if they ate that food, Daniel and his friends would have to break God's laws about some things they weren't allowed to eat. So Daniel asked the king's servant if he and his friends could eat only vegetables for 10 days.

What happened when the 10 days were completed? Read Daniel 1:15 to find out. When 10 days were up, the king's servant could see that they looked healthier than everyone else! Later, at the end of their training, the king, Nebuchadnezzar, thought Daniel and his friends were wiser than anyone in the kingdom! Daniel worked hard for that king for many years.

Years later, King Nebuchadnezzar had a strange and terrible dream. He called for all his wise men. He wanted them to tell what his dream WAS. Besides THAT, Nebuchadnezzar wanted to know what his dream MEANT! WELL! The wise men were ALL going to be killed if they didn't come up with both the dream and its meaning! **What do you think Daniel did? Read Daniel 2:16-18 to see.**

Daniel and his friends prayed. And during the night, God showed Daniel not only what the dream WAS, but He also showed Daniel what it MEANT! Daniel praised God! And of course, when he went to tell the king, Nebuchadnezzar was amazed. **What did Daniel tell Nebuchadnezzar in 2:27-28?** Because Daniel had made a habit of prayer and building his relationship with God, he was trusted to serve God in this unusual way.

Many years later, Nebuchadnezzar's son, Belshazzar, was the king when a VERY strange thing happened. Belshazzar was eating and drinking from beautiful gold cups that had been wrongly taken from God's Temple in Jerusalem. Belshazzar was also making offerings to idols of the false gods he worshiped. Suddenly, a HAND appeared out of NOWHERE! It wrote on a wall some words that no one understood. **Let's read Daniel 5:6 to see how Belshazzar reacted.**

No one knew what those words meant. But the elderly queen remembered Daniel. King Belshazzar called for Daniel. Daniel told the king exactly what the words meant: Belshazzar's time to rule had come to an end. That very night, another king sneaked into Babylon with his armies and took over the whole kingdom!

The new king was named Darius. He must have heard all about Daniel because he made Daniel a very high official in HIS kingdom, too! Daniel did such a good job serving King Darius that the other officials were jealous. They tried to find something wrong that Daniel had done, so they could say bad things to the king about him. But they couldn't find ANYTHING! Daniel was a wise, honest and trustworthy man!

By this time, Daniel was old. He had loved and obeyed God his whole life! He still prayed to God every day with his windows open to Jerusalem, his homeland.

Daniel's prayers gave the jealous officials an idea. **Read Daniel 6:7 to find out their sneaky plan.** The king signed the law. But Daniel prayed—to GOD—as he always did. He wasn't going to change his habit of praying! The other officials brought Daniel to the king and insisted that Daniel be put in the hungry lions' den, because he had broken the king's law. The king did NOT want to do this, but even he couldn't change the law! Daniel had to be thrown into the lions' den!

That night, King Darius didn't sleep. In the morning, he went out to the lions' den to see if Daniel was still alive. **Read Daniel 6:21,22 to see what happened.** The king was overjoyed! God had saved Daniel! The king even made a new law declaring that people should worship Daniel's God.

© 2000 Gospel Light. Permission to photocopy granted. *The Great Stewardship Adventure for Kids*

Conclusion

Daniel was fit to serve God his whole life. He lived wisely, practicing good habits every day, praying and loving and obeying God all his life! Even when it was hard or frightening, Daniel kept on making right choices because he had made a daily habit of obeying God, of praying to God and of spending time with God.

24 GETTING FOCUSED

Every day, from the time we are very young to the time we are very old, we make choices about how we live, too. When we choose to do things that make us able and fit to serve God and practice doing those things, we build good habits that help us become the people God wants us to be.

Use these discussion questions as you lead students in one or more of the Getting Focused activities:

- **When do you think Daniel might have been afraid? What did he do that showed obedience to God?**
- **What are some of the good things Daniel chose to do?**
- **What did Daniel say and do that showed he was a good steward of God's gifts?**
- **What do you think Daniel knew about God that helped him be courageous enough to obey God?**
- **What are things a kid your age can do to become better able to be a good steward for God and please Him?**
- **Is being fit to serve God the same kind of fitness we hear about on TV? How is it the same? different?**
- **What is one habit you can begin to build today? What are ways you could help yourself practice this until it becomes a good habit that helps you every day?**

ACTIVE FOCUS:
Practice Makes Perfect

Materials: Bible with bookmark at Deuteronomy 6:5; discussion questions; masking tape; materials for one or more of the activities below.

Preparation: Set up one or more of the activities below.

Procedure:

1. Read, or ask a volunteer to read, Deuteronomy 6:5. **How did Daniel show he loved God with all of his heart, soul and strength?** Volunteers respond. **What are some of the good habits Daniel had?** (He obeyed God. He prayed to God.) **Because Daniel practiced good habits, he was ready and able to serve God whenever he got the opportunity. We need to practice good habits so that we will be prepared to serve God, too. Let's practice doing something several times to see if we get better at doing it.**

2. Explain activities to the students. Students move around to the different activities as time

© 2000 Gospel Light. Permission to photocopy granted. *The Great Stewardship Adventure for Kids*

allows. Make sure students try the chosen activity more than once so that they get to practice it.

Beanbag Toss: Set a large plastic bowl or tub about 5 feet (1.5 m) from a masking-tape line. Students stand behind line, face away from tub and toss beanbag over shoulder back toward the tub.

Ball Bounce: Place a trash can about 8 feet (2.4 m) away from a masking-tape line. Students stand behind line and throw the ball to bounce it into the trash can. The ball must bounce at least once before it enters the trash can.

Marshmallow Move: Set an open bag of marshmallows and a pair of chopsticks about 4 feet (1.2 m) from a plastic bowl. Students use chopsticks to pick up a marshmallow and carry it to the plastic bowl without touching marshmallow with their hands.

3. Whenever students successfully complete a task, ask them to answer one of the discussion questions. Use the following questions to extend the discussion:

- **Which activity was the hardest at first? the easiest?**
- **Which activity took the most practice for you to get better at?**
- **How did the activities become easier the more you practiced them?**
- **What other activities do you practice?**
- **What could you practice doing each day that would help you be a good steward now? later in life?**

Teaching Tips

1. Let first student in line choose a new way to throw the ball or toss the beanbag. Other students imitate.

2. Create your own activities according to your students' abilities and interests.

Discipline Tip

To avoid discipline problems, carefully explain and demonstrate the rules for each activity and what appropriate behavior will look like. Have students explain the rules again to make sure everyone understands. Also make sure your expectations of student behavior are reasonable for the situation. (Being quiet while throwing beanbags and bouncing balls is extremely difficult.)

ART FOCUS:
Fitness Collage

Materials: Bible with bookmark at Deuteronomy 6:5, discussion questions, butcher paper, measuring stick, masking tape, magazines, scissors, markers, glue.

Preparation: Cut butcher paper into sections about 4-feet (1.2-m) long, one for each group of three to four students. Tape butcher paper sections to wall low enough for kids to work on.

Procedure:

1. Read, or ask a volunteer to read, Deuteronomy 6:5. **What do you think of when you think of loving someone "with all your heart"? "all your soul"? "all your**

© 2000 Gospel Light. Permission to photocopy granted. *The Great Stewardship Adventure for Kids*

strength"? Volunteers respond. **We're going to make a collage to get an idea of some good habits we can practice everyday to prepare us to be good stewards who love God with all their hearts, all their souls and all their strength. What are some things you could look for that would remind you of good habits you could practice?** (Books to remind you to study, a cross to remind you to pray, foods to remind you to eat well, etc.)

2. Divide into groups of three to four students. Assign each group a piece of butcher paper. Students search through magazines to find pictures, words or phrases that remind them of good habits they could practice. Students cut or tear pictures, words or phrases out of magazines, glue them to their group's piece of butcher paper and use markers to add conversation balloons, comments, explanations or decorations.

3. As students work, ask discussion questions. Extend discussion by asking students about the pictures they chose and how the pictures remind them of good habits we can practice every day.

Teaching Tips

At this age, children join together and draw away from adults in the desire for independence. Fourth, fifth and sixth graders enjoy being part of same-gender groups and usually do not want to stand alone in competition. These children no longer automatically talk about whatever they are thinking, so keeping communication open is of prime importance. Listen, ask open-ended questions and avoid being judgmental. Plan learning activities in which students work cooperatively to complete a task. Encouraging boys and girls to be a part of the same small group, even if for a short segment of the session, sometimes helps prevent discipline problems.

FINAL FOCUS

Stewardship Notes

Materials: Bible with bookmark at Deuteronomy 6:5, class notebook, pen.

Procedure: What did we learn today about practicing good habits and being fit to serve God? Ask a volunteer to record students' responses in the class notebook. After students have given answers, volunteer reads aloud from the class notebook a few points from the previous lessons to help students remember what they have learned. **We've learned a lot about stewardship in the last few weeks. How is practicing good habits a part of stewardship?**

Read Deuteronomy 6:5 aloud. **How does this verse describe the way we should love God? When we love God, we want to become members of His family and know Him more.** Talk with interested students about becoming a member of God's family (see "Leading a Student to Christ" on p. 111).

Turning to the prayer journal section of the class notebook, volunteer makes note of prayer requests and answers that students have. To close, pray for the requests given, and then give volunteers an opportunity to say short prayers about whatever is on their hearts. Invite students to pray sentence prayers, thanking God for opportunities to serve Him and asking God's help to practice good habits every day.

 © 2000 Gospel Light. Permission to photocopy granted. *The Great Stewardship Adventure for Kids*

THE LIVING IT! PAGE

SESSION 9

"Love the Lord your God with all your heart and with all your soul and with all your strength."
Deuteronomy 6:5

The Challenge

Daniel 1
When Daniel first came to Babylon, he ate only fruit and vegetables. Unscramble the words in the foods and write them in the matching blanks. When you are done, you'll read about Daniel's life.

corn	watermelon	
peas	mushrooms	pineapple
cherries	orange	asparagus
	grapes	

Look at the picture for 30 seconds. Then turn over your paper and write down all the fruits and vegetables you can remember.

The Super Challenge

NEXT WEEK: GOOD NEWS! Learn about sharing the good news about Jesus.

© 2000 Gospel Light. Permission to photocopy granted. *The Great Stewardship Adventure for Kids*

Topic for Conversation with God

Dear God, please help me make _____ a habit every day.

Running the Race

Eric Liddell was the son of missionaries in China. Because he was ill with a fever for a long time as a child, he wasn't expected to become very strong. At the age of seven he was sent away to a boarding school in England. His parents may have hoped he would get a good education, but they probably never expected him to grow into an athlete. He surprised everyone with his wonderful ability to run like the wind! Eric was more than an athlete, however. He prayed, planned and trained with the goal in mind of being fit for God's service.

He won race after race and was eventually chosen to race in the 1924 Olympics! He trained hard for two races. But when he learned that those races would be held on a Sunday, he announced that he would not dishonor the Lord by running on His day. Instead, he trained for another race, the 400-meter race. Everyone wondered how he would do in a race for which he had not trained very long. How could he risk his chances just so he could honor God, when an Olympic medal was at stake? Eric Liddell not only won a gold medal for the 400-meter race, but he also set a new world record doing it!

Eric not only honored God by his attitude toward sporting events held on Sunday, but he also wanted his whole life to count for God. He saw the need for people to know about Jesus, especially young men. So he used his athletic fame to attract people to meetings where he preached the gospel! And his whole-life fitness didn't stop there. He later returned to China as a missionary. Eventually he was taken captive during a fight between Japan and China, and he died in a Japanese prison camp—a champion for Jesus Christ all his life.

Daily Nuggets

What's better than a habit of biting your fingernails or even brushing your teeth three times a day? Here are some handy helpful habits that will make you ready to serve God:

DAY 1 • Acts 1:14
What did the disciples constantly do together? Who could you do this with?

DAY 2 • Philippians 4:8
What's a good habit for your head?

DAY 3 • Psalm 103:1-5
How can this become a habit? What reasons do these verses give for why we should do this?

DAY 4 • 2 Timothy 3:14-17
What good habit is this verse about? When is a time you could do this each day?

DAY 5 • Hebrews 10:25
What are some ways to form this habit? How does encouraging others help you make this a habit, too?

Family Builder

With your family, decide on a habit you can build together: taking walks, eating meals, reading the Bible, etc. Write out and decorate reminder notes to tape on each family member's bedroom door.

© 2000 Gospel Light. Permission to photocopy granted. *The Great Stewardship Adventure for Kids*

Trusted to Share the Good News

LIFE FOCUS

As good stewards, we can share the treasure of our salvation with others.

1 GETTING PREPARED

AIMS

DISCOVER ways people communicate;
DISCUSS ways to tell others about Jesus;
WRITE examples of words to use when telling others about Jesus.

SCRIPTURE

Acts 8:4-6,26-40

KEY VERSE

"Always be prepared to give an answer to everyone who asks you to give the reason for the hope that you have. But do this with gentleness and respect." 1 Peter 3:15

Teacher's Devotional

Many of us remember when we took the step of faith and chose to follow Jesus. The changes He made in us then, and continues to make in us now, are indeed astounding miracles of grace. We have received His greatest gift—redemption! We receive the mystery of the indwelling of His Holy Spirit. It's impossible to keep the story of that kind of power to ourselves!

   As faithful stewards of God's gifts, it's natural for us to share God's greatest gift, salvation through Jesus. Sharing our testimony with a friend who responds by also trusting Jesus with his or her life can

© 2000 Gospel Light. Permission to photocopy granted. *The Great Stewardship Adventure for Kids*

be one of the most exciting experiences a believer has. To do this naturally and easily, the believer should first give careful thought to his or her own story. Like Philip in today's story, we need to be prepared to respond in any situation "to give the reason for the hope that [we] have" (1 Peter 3.15).

Take time this week to remember the ways God used to bring you into His family. How can you tell your story so that your students will understand it and relate to it? As both you and your students take time during this session to identify the key steps you all have taken in your individual walks of faith, you will each become better prepared to intentionally pray, plan and develop relationships with others through which they can be brought to Christ.

② GETTING STARTED

News Letters

Materials: Slips of paper, markers, paper bag, large sheet of paper.

Procedure: Distribute a slip of paper and a marker to each student. **Print the first letter of your name on the slip of paper.** Collect slips of paper and place in paper bag. **What does it mean to communicate?** (Tell things to others and have them tell things to us.) **Let's think of different ways people communicate.** Each student takes a turn picking a slip of paper from bag. Student tells a way people communicate that begins with the letter on the slip of paper. Guide students to think of nonverbal as well as verbal means of communication (billboard, card, e-mail, expression, frown, letter, magazine, radio, sign language, smile, shake head, TV, whisper, etc.). Student then writes the way he or she mentioned on large sheet of paper. Continue until each student has had a turn or as time permits. **There are a lot of ways that people communicate. Today we will see that communication is a part of stewardship.**

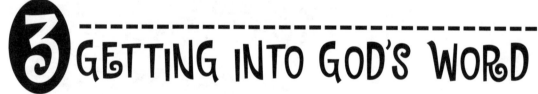

③ GETTING INTO GOD'S WORD

Materials: Bibles.

Bible Study

Students find Acts 8 in their Bibles. As you lead the following study, help students to discover answers in their Bibles.

When was a time you had to explain something to someone else? What made you prepared to help? Volunteers respond. **Today we're going to hear about a man who had to explain something in a very unusual way!**

Philip was a follower of Jesus and willingly helped to do some of the jobs that needed to be done in his church. One of Philip's jobs was to help make sure everyone had enough food to eat (see Acts 6:1-6). The Bible tells us that Philip was chosen for this job because he was full of God's Spirit and was wise. He became wise by praying, studying God's Word and doing what it says. As a result, Philip was ready to do whatever God's Holy Spirit wanted him to do.

People had begun persecuting Christians in Jerusalem, where Philip lived. So many of the Christians moved away to live in different places. Philip was one of those Christians who left Jerusalem.

 © 2000 Gospel Light. Permission to photocopy granted. *The Great Stewardship Adventure for Kids*

Read Acts 8:4,5 to find where Philip went and what he did. Philip's next job was teaching others about Jesus in the country of Samaria. God performed many miracles through Philip there. **What was the result of these miracles? Read verse 6.** The miracles amazed people and they wanted to know more. Philip was glad to tell them the good news about Jesus. Many people in Samaria believed what they heard from Philip and began to follow Jesus, too.

But then, Philip had a particularly unusual job.

First, an ANGEL came to Philip and said, "Go to the southbound road—the one that goes from Jerusalem to Gaza."

Philip might have wondered why God wanted him to go somewhere else, when things were going so well where he was. But that didn't slow him down! Philip immediately obeyed these new instructions. **Read Acts 8:27 to find out who Philip saw coming down this road. How would you describe this man?** This man from Ethiopia was an important official to the queen of Ethiopia. (A eunuch is a man who is physically unable to become a father.) He was the treasurer, in charge of all the queen's money! Because this man had been to Jerusalem to worship God, he must have wanted to know more about God.

How many of you like to read while you are traveling? Well, that's exactly what this Ethiopian official was doing—reading a scroll as his chariot rolled right past Philip.

Suddenly the Holy Spirit said to Philip, "Catch up with that chariot and STAY with it!" So Philip did. While Philip was running alongside the chariot, he heard the official reading aloud from the Old Testament book of Isaiah. Philip asked the man a question. **Find out what Philip's question was by reading Acts 8:30.** (Optional: Ask a volunteer to run in place and read the question in Acts 8:30. Volunteer keeps running while you continue with the next part of the story.)

"How can I figure this out unless someone helps me?" the Ethiopian asked. He stopped his chariot and invited Philip to ride with him. Philip was probably glad he didn't have to keep running! (Volunteer stops running.) The two men continued talking. **Read Acts 8:32-34 to find out what puzzled the Ethiopian official.**

"Is this prophet talking about himself or someone else?" the Ethiopian official asked.

Philip knew this passage was describing Jesus, so Philip was prepared to explain this passage and tell the good news about Jesus. **What things do you think Philip said?**

The Ethiopian believed everything that Philip told him about Jesus! This was exactly what he had wanted to understand! Suddenly he saw some water up ahead.

"Here's some water—I could be baptized right now!" the Ethiopian exclaimed. He wanted to show that he wanted to follow Jesus.

So then and there, Philip baptized the man to show he believed that Jesus had died so that sins could be forgiven.

As Philip and the Ethiopian came up out of the water, God's Spirit took Philip to the city of Azotus where he continued to explain God's Word to people and to tell the good news about Jesus. The Ethiopian man didn't see Philip again. **How does Acts 8:39 describe the feelings of the Ethiopian after his baptism?** He continued on his way a happy man, thanking God for loving him and bringing him into God's family.

Conclusion

Philip showed he was a good steward by being ready and willing to explain verses from the Bible—even when it meant running fast enough to catch up to a chariot! He

© 2000 Gospel Light. Permission to photocopy granted. *The Great Stewardship Adventure for Kids*

could share the good news because he had learned about God's Word and was prepared to give the reason for his hope in Jesus. As good stewards we can be prepared to tell others about Jesus, too!

GETTING FOCUSED

Use these discussion questions as you lead students in one or more of the Getting Focused activities:

- **What do you think Philip must have done so that he was ready to share the good news of God's love and forgiveness in Jesus?**
- **What are some of the ways Philip proved he was willing to do whatever God asked him to do?** (Philip made sure people had enough food. He left for the southbound road when the angel told him to. He ran alongside the chariot to talk to the Ethiopian.)
- **Why do you think Philip obeyed immediately when the angel told him to go down a certain road?**
- **What do you think might have happened if Philip had not known how to explain the Bible verses to the Ethiopian?**
- **Tell as many ways as you can how God made it possible for this Ethiopian man to learn about Jesus.**
- **Why do you think kids your age might need someone to explain parts of God's Word to them? Why might it be hard for people to understand the Bible?**
- **What are some ways you can learn more about God's Word?**
- **What are ways kids your age can tell others about Jesus? What words could you use to tell someone else about Jesus? What actions could you use to tell someone else about Jesus?**
- **What are some ways you can be prepared to tell someone the good news?**
- **Why is being prepared to tell others about Jesus a part of good stewardship?**

ACTIVE FOCUS:
Answer Acrostic

Materials: Bible with bookmark at 1 Peter 3:15, discussion questions, graph paper, pencils.

Preparation: Number the columns of a sample grid as described below. Print the word "stewardship" vertically in the center column.

Procedure:

1. Read, or ask a volunteer to read, 1 Peter 3:15 aloud. **What does the verse mean by "the hope that you have"?** (The hope that comes from believing in Jesus and becoming a member of God's family.) **Today we're going to write some words that will help us be prepared to give an answer to anyone who asks why we believe in Jesus.**

2. Divide the class into teams of two or three students each. Give each team a sheet of graph paper and a pencil. Instruct students to locate the center column on the page and write a 0 (zero) at the top. At the top of the first column to the right of the center, they write 5, then 10 at the top of the next and then 15, 20, 25, etc. out to the end of the grid. At the top of the first column to the

© 2000 Gospel Light. Permission to photocopy granted. *The Great Stewardship Adventure for Kids*

left of the center, they write 1 and then 2, 3, 4, 5, etc. out to the end of the grid. Have each team print the word "stewardship" vertically in the center column.

9	8	7	6	5	4	3	2	1	0	5	10	15	20	25	30	35	40	45	50
									s	i	n	n	e	r					
									E	t	h	i	o	p	i	a	n		
									J	e	s	u	s						
									w	o	r	s	h	i	p				
									a	n	s	w	e	r					
								f	o	r	g	i	v	e	n	e	s	s	
							L	o	r	d									
									s	a	l	v	a	t	i	o	n		
									h	o	p	e							
						C	h	r	i	s	t								
									P	h	i	l	i	p					

3. Teams write on their grid important words from the story, words from the key verse or words they could use when telling others about Jesus. Each word must use one of the letters from the word "stewardship" in the center column. Every letter counts points, so long words are more valuable than short ones. Also, more points are scored for letters to the right of the center column than for letters to the left of the center column, so it is better to think of words that begin with the letters in the word "stewardship" than words that end with those letters.

4. As teams work, use discussion questions to encourage conversation and to help students think of words to use in their acrostics. When time is up, teams total their scores. (Example in sketch is worth 922 points.) Each student on the team with the highest score chooses one word from their acrostic and tells how that word could be used to tell others about Jesus.

Teaching Tip
Noticing when a student does something right and acknowledging what you see is often harder than noticing disruptive behavior! Think about how you react when someone points out what you are doing well compared to when someone points out what you are doing wrong. Note a student's good behavior by making comments such as "I see you let Kyle go first. Thank you, Ryan."

ART FOCUS:
Spread-the-News Book

Materials: Bible with bookmark at 1 Peter 3:15, discussion questions, plain paper, scissors, markers.
Preparation: Make a sample book following the directions below.
Procedure:
1. Read, or ask a volunteer to read, 1 Peter 3:15. **What does this verse tell us we should be prepared to do?** (We should be prepared to explain to people why we believe in Jesus.) **What are some things you do to prepare to give answers or explanations in school?** (Study. Read books. Ask other people questions.) Show book you prepared. **Today we're going to make books to help us prepare to tell why we believe in Jesus.**

2. Follow the directions given in the sketches to direct students as they form their books.

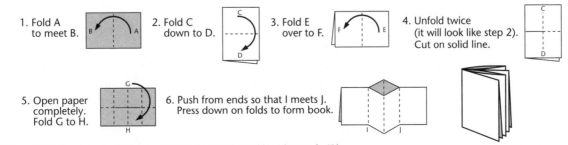

1. Fold A to meet B.
2. Fold C down to D.
3. Fold E over to F.
4. Unfold twice (it will look like step 2). Cut on solid line.
5. Open paper completely. Fold G to H.
6. Push from ends so that I meets J. Press down on folds to form book.

© 2000 Gospel Light. Permission to photocopy granted. *The Great Stewardship Adventure for Kids*

3. After the book is formed, students write a title on the cover. Suggest the students print the following verses, one on each page: 1 John 4:8, Romans 3:23, 1 Corinthians 15:3, 1 John 1:9, Acts 10:43, 1 John 3:1. John 3:16 can be written on the back cover. Students look up and read each verse, and then choose to draw illustrations or write slogans based on the verse on each page.

4. As students work, ask the discussion questions to extend the conversation about telling others about Jesus.

Enrichment Ideas

1. Students use colored paper. Provide extra sheets of paper, plain or colored, for students who want to make additional books.

2. Provide additional materials for students to use in decorating their books: rubber stamps, stickers, glitter pens, yarn, ribbon, glue.

FINAL FOCUS

Stewardship Notes

Materials: Bible with bookmark at 1 Peter 3:15, class notebook, pen.

Procedure: What did we learn today about telling other people about Jesus? Ask a volunteer to record students' responses in the class notebook and read a few notes made during previous sessions to help students review what they have learned, reading ideas from today's session last.

Take a few moments to recite with students today's key verse, 1 Peter 3:15. **What attitude are we supposed to have when we tell others about Jesus?** (We are to show gentleness and respect.) **Sharing the book you made with others is one gentle and respectful way to explain why you believe in Jesus.**

Turning to the prayer journal section of the class notebook, make note of prayer requests and answers that students have. Let's take a few minutes to silently thank God for His love and that He gave us Jesus to be our Savior so that we could become members of His family. Close prayer with the prayer requests and by asking for God's help to tell others about Him.

© 2000 Gospel Light. Permission to photocopy granted. *The Great Stewardship Adventure for Kids*

THE LIVING IT! PAGE

SESSION 10

KEY VERSE

"Always be prepared to give an answer to everyone who asks you to give the reason for the hope that you have. But do this with gentleness and respect." 1 Peter 3:15

Acts 8:26-40

The Challenge

Philip is on his way to the Ethiopian man, but Philip is not sure where to look. See if you can help him. Trace his path from dot to dot so you can do the Super Challenge.

1. Start at the building that is 1 bar tall.
2. Go to the nearest palm tree.
3. Count the rocks under it. Go west that many bars. Then go south.
4. When you reach a tent, go east 2½ bars.
5. At the cave, turn and go north until you reach a building.
6. Go to the nearest sheep.
7. Head southwest 3 bars.
8. Congratulations! You've found the Ethiopian! Where is he? _____

If you found the Ethiopian correctly, write the letters next to the landmarks as you went and you'll discover what Phillip told the Ethiopian about Jesus.

Topic for Conversation with God

God, please help me to know what to say and when to talk to _____ about You!

W · E · N · S

1 bar

ETHIOPIA
JERUSALEM

S · F · O · A · R · O · P · L · N · D · H · C · G · I

The Super Challenge

NEXT WEEK: GOD'S BIG BODY. What can we do together?

© 2000 Gospel Light. Permission to photocopy granted. *The Great Stewardship Adventure for Kids*

© 2000 Gospel Light. Permission to photocopy granted. *The Great Stewardship Adventure for Kids*

SCARY to SHARE!

We all know that we should tell our non-Christian friends and family members about Jesus. But it can be scary to share our faith with others. Here are several fun brain teasers that might help ease the tension. The object of these puzzlers is to turn the word at the top of each column into the word at the bottom. You do this by changing one letter at a time, each time forming a new word—a REAL word (see our example). In each puzzle, we've given you the proper amount of blank lines to fill in. However, most puzzles have more than one solution—you may have to try your own ideas. Example: **SCARY SCARE SHARE** And that's how you change "scary" into "share"!

OK, now you try. Change "give" to "life" (as in give away your faith so that another can have eternal life).

```
G I V E
_ _ _ _
_ _ _ _
L I F E
```

Help someone find "joy" in knowing "God":

```
J O Y
_ _ _
_ _ _
G O D
```

Say "yes" to the "Son" of God:

```
Y E S
_ _ _
_ _ _
_ _ _
_ _ _
S O N
```

Because we "love" God, we want to "tell" others about Him:

```
L O V E
_ _ _ _
_ _ _ _
_ _ _ _
_ _ _ _
T E L L
```

The answer is "live." Simple, eh? Well, sometimes it's not so easy. You'll find out when you try these other ones.

Finally, let God turn your "fear" into the power to "tell" others:

```
F E A R
_ _ _ _
_ _ _ _
_ _ _ _
T E L L
```

Daily Nuggets

God wants us to tell others about Him, so quick—quote at least three verses you could use to explain about God to someone who wants to know! Stumped? HERE'S HELP!!

DAY 1
Why doesn't everybody go to heaven? (CHECK OUT **John 3:16; 6:40** and **Acts 2:37,38**) What do these verses say people need to do to go there? See if you can explain this to a parent or friend.

DAY 2
What's the problem with sin? Check out **Romans 6:23**. What are wages? What gift does this verse promise us?

DAY 3
Why did Jesus come to earth? (See **Luke 19:10**!)

DAY 4
Read **Ephesians 2:8,9**. How are you saved? What kind of work can you do to earn God's gift of salvation?

DAY 5
Read **2 Corinthians 5:14,15,17**. Now you know how to be a completely new creation! What if you blow it and sin? Read **1 John 1:9**.

The Outsider Who Loved Outsiders

In Japan, by the time Toyohiko Kagawa was four years old, both his parents had died. He spent six years with a grandmother who didn't want to take care of him. Many times, he felt so unloved and uncared for, he wished he were dead. He struggled through his younger years and finally an older brother took him to a school where he could learn English. It was a mission school, and it was here that Toyohiko learned about Jesus, the outsider who was rejected and killed but who loved people like no one else ever had. Toyohiko came to love this Jesus!

Toyohiko's first prayer was "Oh, God, make me like Jesus!" God answered that prayer in wonderful ways. Toyohiko stayed in school and studied hard. Although he still felt like an outsider, he knew Jesus loved and cared for him. He began to help the homeless beggars that seemed to be everywhere. He decided that to be like Jesus and share the good news of Jesus with these people, he needed to move to the slums where they lived. So he moved to the slums; and he preached there and gave medical help, food and whatever he had to help those around him. He told others about Jesus not only through his words but also by his actions. Over the years, he made such changes in the slums that he became well known in Japan and was invited to America to learn more ways to help his people.

During World War II, much of Japan was destroyed. Toyohiko was called on by his government to help them put things back together. His work in the slums had trained him for just that kind of work. He was eager to help and to share the good news of Jesus with all who would listen. Even the emperor of Japan sought to learn about Toyohiko's amazing friend Jesus—the One who made his life worth living.

Together, Much Can Be Accomplished

LIFE FOCUS

Good stewards make use of everyone's gifts to serve God and others.

1 GETTING PREPARED

AIMS

DISCOVER that by working with others we can do things we can't do alone;
RECOGNIZE ways of serving God and others when we use our gifts together;
SERVE others by working together.

SCRIPTURE

Nehemiah 1—4

KEY VERSE

"Now you are the body of Christ, and each one of you is a part of it." 1 Corinthians 12:27

Teacher's Devotional

We read the account in Nehemiah of rebuilding the wall around Jerusalem. The wall had broken down, and the people used the fallen stones to restore the wall to its former height and strength. Rebuilding the wall was not a task to be taken lightly. It wasn't a weekend's work; it required weeks of labor. And it was not a task that Nehemiah planned to do alone. Nehemiah's first order of business after assessing the damage was to call the remaining inhabitants of Jerusalem together and place them, by family, in strategic locations to begin rebuilding sections of the wall. Even when opposition came and the people were discouraged, God kept them going, largely through the encouragement and leadership of Nehemiah and Ezra.

© 2000 Gospel Light. Permission to photocopy granted. *The Great Stewardship Adventure for Kids*

In much the same way, we as the body of Christ can do much to serve God and others by working together. Whatever our job in the church, whether it's teaching a Sunday School class, cleaning the bathrooms, singing in the choir or counting the offering money, we need to understand that it's the combined efforts that keep the church going. No one person's job is more important than anyone else's job. They are all necessary. It's a stone-on-stone, day-by-day work that requires faithfulness and patience. When God's people unite, the synergy and accomplishment can be amazing! Help your students understand that God made us a body so that we can work together to accomplish far more together than we ever could alone!

2 GETTING STARTED

Together Tasks

Materials: Measuring stick, rope.

Procedure: Students work together to accomplish one or both of the following tasks.

Long Long Jump: Students line up single file. First student in line jumps as far as he or she can. Next student in line jumps from the spot where the first student landed. Continue in the same manner until all students have added to the long jump. Measure the total distance. Repeat activity to see if students can extend the distance. (Divide large classes into groups to complete this activity.)

Tug-of-Peace: Students sit in a circle. Provide a strong rope tied to make a loop. Rope's length should be approximately 1 foot (30 cm) for each student. Students grab hold of the rope and pull themselves to a standing position. (When everyone works together and pulls at the same time, students should be able to stand up together.)

Could anyone ever jump as far alone as you did working together? What made it easy or difficult to pull yourselves up by pulling on the rope? Volunteers respond. **Some things are done better when people work together. What kinds of tasks are easier to do with someone else than by yourself? In our lesson today, we'll find out ways of serving God and others by using our gifts together.**

3 GETTING INTO GOD'S WORD

Materials: Bibles.

Bible Study

Students find Nehemiah 1—4 in their Bibles. As you lead the following study, help students to discover answers in their Bibles.

When was a time you had a really big project to do? What kind of help did you get to finish the project? Volunteers respond. **Today we're going to hear about someone who had a really big project to do.**

What would you say is the most important place in our city? In Bible times, a city's WALL was very important. The wall surrounded the city, keeping the people inside safe from

© 2000 Gospel Light. Permission to photocopy granted. *The Great Stewardship Adventure for Kids*

attackers and wild animals. The wall was the first thing visitors would see. So in Bible times, a strong and beautiful city wall was very important.

About 500 years before Jesus was born, many Israelites were living in a land called Persia, far away from Jerusalem. One of these Israelites was Nehemiah, a servant to the king of Persia. Some of Nehemiah's relatives still lived in Jerusalem, a city that had once had a great, high, strong wall.

No matter how far away he lived, Nehemiah considered Jerusalem his real home. When he heard that the wall of Jerusalem was broken down and the people were in great trouble, he was so upset he cried! For several days Nehemiah went without food; he prayed that God would help him gain the king's favor toward repairing the wall in Jerusalem.

When the king of Persia saw Nehemiah, he could tell something was wrong. "Nehemiah, why do you look so sad?" the king asked Nehemiah. **Read Nehemiah 2:2-3 to find out how Nehemiah felt and what he said.** Even though Nehemiah was afraid, he knew God had given him this opportunity to ask for the king's help.

Nehemiah said a silent prayer. Then he took a deep breath. "I'd like you to send me to Jerusalem to rebuild the city wall," Nehemiah said. **To find out what the king said, read Nehemiah 2:6.**

Nehemiah eagerly made arrangements and then set off for Jerusalem. He was accompanied by soldiers on horses and by letters from the king for supplies.

Nehemiah traveled for many days. Finally, he could see the formerly beautiful Jerusalem—now, not so beautiful. Nehemiah's heart sank as he rode around the rubble and ruins that were supposed to be the city's wall. Without the wall for protection, the people lived in constant fear of being attacked.

Nehemiah set to work right away. First, he talked to the people. For the wall to be rebuilt, Nehemiah needed everyone's help! Nehemiah assured them that GOD wanted them to rebuild the wall. With God's help, NO ONE could keep them from getting the job done.

Of course, some people—people who wanted to be able to attack the city whenever they felt like it—didn't want the wall to be rebuilt! So they did everything they could think of to STOP the Israelites from rebuilding the wall.

Their first plan was to make fun of the Israelites. "You weaklings! What makes you think you can do anything, let alone build a wall to keep us out?" the enemies taunted. "Look at what you're trying to build with. Those rocks are burned and worthless, just like you. Why, even a fox standing on that wall would break it down!"

The people of Jerusalem didn't need their enemies insulting them, trying to make them give up. **Read Nehemiah 4:4. What did Nehemiah ask God to do?** Nehemiah didn't waste time or energy trying to get even with his enemies. He trusted God to take care of everything. And he encouraged the people to keep on working together.

Soon Nehemiah's enemies came up with a new plot. Since the people of Jerusalem were already halfway finished with the building of the wall, the enemies planned to attack Jerusalem before the wall was any higher. Again, Nehemiah prayed to God for help. Nehemiah then posted a guard to watch over the workers.

Nehemiah may have remained confident in God's help, but the people of Jerusalem were getting worried AND they were getting tired. "Maybe our enemies are right. Maybe this is an impossible task," the people grumbled. **What did Nehemiah say to reassure the people? Read Nehemiah 4:14. How do you think the people responded?**

Nehemiah then set up another plan to make sure the workers were safe. **Read Nehemiah 4:16-18 to find out what Nehemiah planned to do.** When the enemies heard about what had happened, they went away—at least for a while.

© 2000 Gospel Light. Permission to photocopy granted. *The Great Stewardship Adventure for Kids*

Conclusion

In spite of their difficulties, it took Nehemiah and his workers only 52 days to rebuild the wall of Jerusalem! (See Nehemiah 6:15.) **Without Nehemiah, the people of Jerusalem might never have had the courage to even TRY to rebuild the wall. With Nehemiah's prayers and plans leading them, the people not only rebuilt the wall, but they also learned that if they worked together and depended on God for help, what may seem impossible to do, CAN be done!**

24 GETTING FOCUSED

Use these discussion questions as you lead students in one or more of the Getting Focused activities:

- **What were some problems Nehemiah had in rebuilding the wall around Jerusalem?**
- **What did Nehemiah do about the problems?** (He prayed to God. He made a plan. He took action. He got other people to help him.) **How did Nehemiah show good stewardship of God's gifts?**
- **How did everyone work together? What different skills do you think were needed to rebuild the wall?**
- **What do you think might have happened if the people were not willing to work together when things got difficult?**
- **How does praying together about problems help? Why?**
- **When are some times that it may be hard for a kid your age to work together with others? What can be done to make each time easier?**
- **What are some ways that the members of God's family work together to serve others? What are some ways you could work with other kids your age to serve God?**
- **How does working with others as part of a team show good stewardship?** (Other people are a gift from God. When we work with them wisely, we can accomplish a good deal. It helps each person use his or her abilities in the best way.)

ART FOCUS:
Together Art

Materials: Bibles, discussion questions, large sheets of construction paper, markers, tape.
Procedure:

1. Students form groups of three. After reading 1 Corinthians 12:27, each group works together to make a poster of the verse. **Your poster should show which words in the verse you think are most important. What are some ways you might show the important words?** (Underline them. Write them in a different color. Write them in capital letters. Draw pictures to go with the words.) **What are some of the different jobs that will be needed to finish the poster?** (Someone will have to get construction paper and markers. Someone will do the printing of the verse.) Students in each group plan a way to illustrate poster, decide who will do the different tasks and then work together to make their group's poster.

© 2000 Gospel Light. Permission to photocopy granted. *The Great Stewardship Adventure for Kids*

2. After posters are completed, each group tapes poster to classroom wall. Discuss the key words identified on each poster. **Why is this word important? What does this verse tell you about God's family?** (We're all important. We need each other. We can't do everything on our own.) Allow time for each group to respond. **How does working with others show good stewardship?** (We can do more with the gifts and abilities God has given us when we combine them with the gifts God has given others.) **What are some things you could do as a team that would serve others?** Ask the discussion questions to extend your conversation with students.

Teaching Tip

As students work together, talk with them about how important it is for each person to use his or her abilities and to work cooperatively together. **What kinds of jobs at school or at home are easily accomplished when everyone uses their abilities together?**

Discipline Tip

Recognize accomplishments and good behavior. "I really appreciated how you . . ." or "You're really good at . . ." are two ways to affirm your students. Encourage all children, not only those who are often behavior problems but also those who have already achieved a high degree of self-control. When children know they will receive attention for positive behavior, their display of disruptive behavior often diminishes.

SERVICE FOCUS: Building Up the Body

Materials: Bible with bookmark at 1 Corinthians 12:27, discussion questions, materials for the project you choose.

Procedure:

1. Read, or ask a volunteer to read, 1 Corinthians 12:27. **This verse compares all the members of God's family to the different parts of a body. This means that we are all a part of a team that works together! When are some times that you have been a part of a team?** Volunteers respond.

2. Choose one of the following projects to help your church family, or do a different project that meets a need in your church.

Good as New Crayons: Collect crayon stubs from younger children's classrooms. Sort colors. Students remove paper and break crayons into small pieces. Keeping colors separate, put broken crayons in old muffin tins and place in oven on low temperature. (Optional: Put crayons in small paper cups and heat in microwave.) Allow crayons to melt. Remove from oven. When crayons are hardened and cool, remove from muffin tins and give to classrooms where crayon stubs were collected. (Always supervise students when using an oven. Provide hot pads and oven mitts for students to use when handling hot materials. Caution students to be careful not to touch or spill the melted wax as it will be very hot.)

Sidewalk Chalk: Mix powdered tempera paint with ½ cup water and 3 tablespoons plaster of paris. Pour the mixture into a small paper cup. Allow to dry; then peel off the cup. Give to a pre-school class to use outside as sidewalk chalk.

Trash Collectors: Give trash bags to groups of two or three students. Students collect trash from church parking lot or from the church grounds. If possible, pick up trash in a nearby park or community area. Provide students with inexpensive gloves to diminish risk of contact with contaminated materials. Allow time for students to wash hands at the end of the activity.

3. As students work, promote discussion of ways to work together to serve others. **The people we work with are gifts from God to help us. We practice good stewardship when we work with others. Plus, we can do more to serve God and others when we combine our gifts from God! What are some other things you could work on together to serve others?** Volunteers respond. Ask the discussion questions to further extend the discussion.

Enrichment Tip

Students experiment with making multicolored crayons or chalk.

Learning Tip

Kids don't always remember everything we say, but they learn quite a bit from what we do and how we react. Your enthusiasm for wanting to help others will speak volumes more than saying "Now we are going to do something important." If you approach service projects with the attitude that this is something you HAVE to do, instead of something you WANT to do, your students will learn that Christian service is a drudgery. To be servants of our King is the greatest privilege we have! Don't be afraid to let your enthusiasm show. Tell why you want to do this and how others will benefit from it. Then your students will learn that Christian service is a joy!

FINAL FOCUS

Stewardship Notes

Materials: Bible with bookmark at 1 Corinthians 12:27, class notebook, pen.

Procedure: What did we learn today about working together? Ask a volunteer to record students' ideas and comments in the class notebook and read a few notes made during previous sessions to help students review what they have learned, reading ideas from today's session last.

Take a few moments to recite with students today's key verse, 1 Corinthians 12:27. **What does this verse tell us we are all members of? How is working together a part of stewardship?**

Turning to the prayer journal section of the class notebook, make note of prayer requests and answers that students have. Ask volunteers to share ideas about ways to work together to serve others. **Let's take a few minutes to thank God for giving us other people to work with.** Students pray short prayers thanking God for the people He has given us and for prayer requests. Close by asking for God's help to find ways to use our gifts to serve Him and others.

© 2000 Gospel Light. Permission to photocopy granted. *The Great Stewardship Adventure for Kids*

SESSION 11

1 Corinthians 12:27

The Challenge

These kids have built a big wall that's hiding the Bible verse. Follow the instructions to read the verse. Write the leftover words in order on the blank lines.

STEP 1: Cross out all the names of colors.

STEP 2: Cross out all the types of transportation.

STEP 3: Lose the girls' names.

STEP 4: Hey, why pick on the girls? Cross out the boys' names, too.

STEP 5: Who needs the names of different toys? You don't.

STEP 6: Finally, let's get rid of the school subjects. (Hey, it's only for this puzzle!)

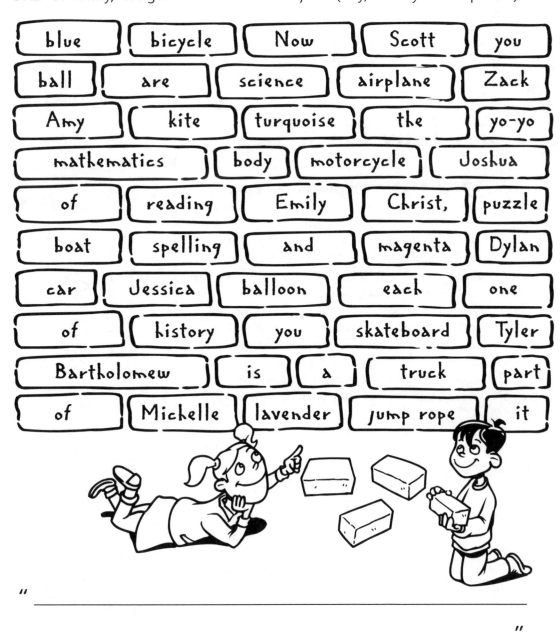

blue	bicycle	Now	Scott	you
ball	are	science	airplane	Zack
Amy	kite	turquoise	the	yo-yo
mathematics	body	motorcycle	Joshua	
of	reading	Emily	Christ,	puzzle
boat	spelling	and	magenta	Dylan
car	Jessica	balloon	each	one
of	history	you	skateboard	Tyler
Bartholomew	is	a	truck	part
of	Michelle	lavender	jump rope	it

NEXT WEEK: SHARE!
Why should you care to share?

KEY VERSE
"Now you are the body of Christ, and each one of you is a part of it." 1 Corinthians 12:27

"_____

_____."

© 2000 Gospel Light. Permission to photocopy granted. *The Great Stewardship Adventure for Kids*

Daily Nuggets

So many different people, all in one church! So many churches, all serving one God! Find out what Paul said about working together as ONE BODY.

DAY 1: 1 Corinthians 12:12-20
What does Paul compare the church to? What can an eye do that an ear can't? Why are both necessary?

DAY 2: Ephesians 4:15,16
Who is the head of the Body? How does the Body grow or build itself up?

DAY 3: Romans 12:4-8
What are some of the jobs members of the Body of Christ can have? Which of these jobs can you do?

DAY 4: 1 Timothy 4:12
No one is too young to make a difference in the Body of Christ! How can you set a good example for others?

DAY 5: Colossians 3:15-17
What are some of the jobs listed in these verses? What are we to give to God in everything we do?

BONUS: John 17:20-23
Who was Jesus praying for? What did Jesus pray would happen?

Discovery and Exploration

What are some ways your church helps people in your community? How could you become involved?

Family Builder

Plan a cooperative meal this week. Assign one part of the meal to each family member to complete. Invite another family to your home to share the meal!

A House of Many Hands

When Andrea's dad moved out, her mother, Carrie, could no longer afford to keep their home. Andrea and her mom had no place to live. At first they stayed with friends; but being "couch hoppers," as Carrie called it, became hopeless. Finally, Carrie found a room to rent that they could afford. It was a tight fit—and there were too many bugs and lice. They didn't stay. Another place Carrie found turned out to be miserable, too. They kept moving, hoping to find a place where they could live and begin to rebuild their lives. Finally Carrie heard about a house that was FREE for moms and kids who were homeless. It was supported by members of a church and some other people who had worked together to pay for and provide this house. Carrie and Andrea were so excited! The house was clean! It was nice! And they could AFFORD to live there! They moved in. While Carrie studied at a nearby college, the house became their home! The two of them felt safe and secure again, in a place where they could "rebuild the walls" of their lives.

While Andrea and Carrie lived at the house, the directors planned to build another, larger house for homeless women and children, so they could help four or five families at a time. Now that big yellow house stands completed—built mainly by a volunteer construction crew. Many Christians worked together to build a place where there is help and encouragement for women and children who are homeless. Just like Nehemiah's wall-rebuilding, the big yellow house became a reality because many of God's people helped.

Today, Andrea and Carrie have rebuilt lives. Carrie now has a college degree and works in the big yellow house. Their lives have changed in wonderful ways because many people worked together to build houses and help rebuild lives.

Topic for Conversation with God

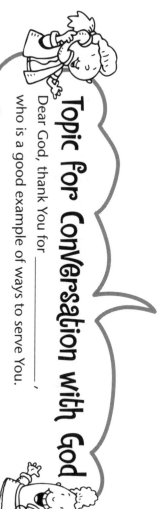

Dear God, thank You for _____, who is a good example of ways to serve You.

94

© 2000 Gospel Light. Permission to photocopy granted. *The Great Stewardship Adventure for Kids*

Share and Share Alike

LIFE FOCUS

As good stewards, we can share the gifts that God has given to us.

1 GETTING PREPARED

AIMS

IDENTIFY things that we can share with others;
IDENTIFY different ways to share with others;
DISCUSS ways to share God's gifts with others.

SCRIPTURE

Acts 2:14-47; 4:32-35; 5:12-16; 6:1-7

KEY VERSE

"All the believers were one in heart and mind. No one claimed that any of his possessions was his own, but they shared everything they had." Acts 4:32

Teacher's Devotional

The account of the Early Church compels us to examine our own stewardship. As faithful, responsible and loving members of God's family, as people who say we trust God for all we need, how should we live? The story of the Early Church holds a mysterious sweetness—everything was held in common and no one claimed sole ownership over anything. It is a mystery to us because we generally can't imagine how it could work in any practical way today, yet it is sweet because we'd like to imagine a world or even a church where there are no people in need.

This story shows us how to handle surplus: first, it demonstrates how we can trust God to supply more than we need; second, it shows us how we can use the surplus with which God has supplied

© 2000 Gospel Light. Permission to photocopy granted. *The Great Stewardship Adventure for Kids*

to us. In the Early Church, all they needed was a mechanism to organize the movement of that surplus into the hands of those who needed it. God directed them to choose godly men to oversee this work. This moving of the surplus was a valued and important way to honor every member of God's family with what they needed. Think about the mechanisms that are in place in your own church to help move surplus to those who need it. Think of how to help your students see that there is a joy they may have never before experienced that results when we sacrifice our goods and give freely of our surplus. It's the way of God's family—then and now!

② GETTING STARTED

Sharing Charades

Materials: Index cards, markers.

Preparation: Print the following words on separate index cards: "love," "friendship," "God" and "The Bible."

Procedure: Distribute a blank index card and a marker to each student. **Without talking with anyone else, write the name of something that you could share with others on your index card.** Collect index cards from students and mix with the cards you prepared. Students take turns picking out a card and acting out the word written on it without saying any words. Students guess what is being acted out until the word is identified. Continue until each student has a turn or as time allows. **These are all things that we know we can share with others. Today we're going to learn about different ways we, as stewards, can share with others.**

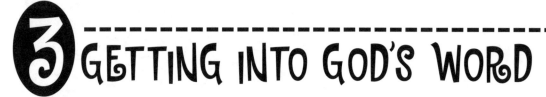

③ GETTING INTO GOD'S WORD

Materials: Bibles.

Bible Study

Students find the book of Acts in their Bibles. As you lead the following study, help students to discover answers in their Bibles.

Tell about a time when someone shared something with you. What did that person share? Was it easy for the person to share or was it difficult? Today we'll meet some people who did a LOT of sharing!

After Jesus returned to heaven, God sent His Holy Spirit to the followers of Jesus. **How many people became part of God's family? Read Acts 2:41 to find out.** What a BIG family! But it was only the BEGINNING of this family we now call the Church.

Every day after that, the members of God's family came together to listen to the teachings of Jesus' followers. They met together at the Temple or in each other's homes and they sang praises, prayed and read and talked about God's Word. They worshiped God with all their hearts. They were glad to be together!

What's another thing these members of God's family did? Read Acts 4:32. The

© 2000 Gospel Light. Permission to photocopy granted. *The Great Stewardship Adventure for Kids*

members of the Early Church loved God and each other so much, they shared everything they had with each other. Nobody said, "That's MINE!" about anything. Everything they had, they shared with the other members of God's family. They took good care of each other. **What is one way they did this? Read Acts 4:34 to find out.**

In order to take care of the members of God's family who were poor, some of the wealthier people would sell their land or other belongings. Then they would bring the money to the apostles and hand it ALL over to them! The apostles would then give the money to anyone in God's family who needed it. The members of the Early Church wanted to please God by caring for each other. They made sure that no one in God's family was hungry or needed anything. They followed Jesus' example to love and obey God and take care of others.

When the members of God's family met together to worship God at the Temple in Jerusalem, many people who didn't believe in Jesus were coming to the Temple, too. These people had a great deal of respect for the members of the Church, and they heard the teachings of God's followers. **Read Acts 5:14 to find out what happened to these people.** They believed in Jesus and became members of God's family, too!

This big family grew and grew, and they loved each other in a BIG way! But in this growing family of God, there was a special need. Many widows (women whose husbands had died) needed help. In those days, women couldn't go out and get jobs. These widows needed help to feed themselves and their children. The church collected food and money to give to widows.

But some of the needy widows were not from Jerusalem. They were from countries where the people spoke Greek. And the Greek widows weren't getting as much food as the widows who had always lived in Jerusalem. These Greek widows could have gotten angry and quit meeting with the church. But instead they told the disciples about their problem.

The disciples did NOT want these widows to think the other people in God's family didn't care about them! So they called a meeting to solve the problem. **How do you think they solved this problem? Read Acts 6:3 to find out.**

They said, "We need people who will make sure no one goes hungry. We want to be sure we share equally with everyone in God's family. Let's choose some people who can make sure everyone gets enough food."

Everyone in the meeting was happy with this solution, and the disciples chose seven men. **Read Acts 6:5 to find out about these men. How is Stephen described?** Nicolas is described as a convert to Judaism. That means he had grown up speaking Greek and following Greek customs. In fact, all seven of the men have Greek names. **Why do you think it was important that the men chosen to solve the problem were all Greek?** The Greek widows were probably reassured to know that the people who were in charge of food distribution were from the same country as they were from.

The leaders of the church put their hands on the seven men as a symbol of their approval and asked God to give the men all that they needed to do their task. Then these men made sure that the food and other things were shared with ALL the widows fairly. The Greek word used to describe the job of these seven men is the same word that the word "deacon" comes from. Many churches today choose or elect deacons whose job is to help take care of practical needs (like food) in the church.

What happened next in Jerusalem? Read Acts 6:7. What might have happened in this church if the problem between the Greek and Hebrew widows had not been solved? The church grew and grew. It became known as a welcoming place where God's love was not only talked about, but it was also demonstrated by the way the people shared all they had with each other.

Conclusion

We're part of the same Church as the one we read about in the book of Acts. The reason we come together is because we want to share our love for God, learn more about Him and share the gifts God has given to us with others. By sharing with others, we are practicing good stewardship of God's gifts.

24 GETTING FOCUSED

Use these discussion questions as you lead students in one or more of the Getting Focused activities:

- **What are ways the people in the Early Church helped each other? What things did they share?**
- **What did the actions of God's family show to others? Would you have liked to have these people as your friends? Why?**
- **When has a person you know shown love for God by helping or caring for someone else? What did that person share?**
- **What are some of the ways members of God's family have shared with you?**
- **What are ways you could share things God has given to you with other members of God's family? with people who are not members of God's family?** (In addition to sharing food and other good things God has given us, we can share what we know about Jesus.)
- **What can people share besides money and food?**
- **What are some things that might happen when a kid your age is selfish?**
- **What are ways we can be generous and share in this classroom? What's a way you could share with another member of our class this week? at home with a family member? at school?**

ACTIVE FOCUS: Quick Quote

Materials: Bible with bookmark at Acts 4:32, discussion questions, large sheet of paper, markers, masking tape, index cards.

Preparation: Print the words of Acts 4:32 on large sheet of paper. Tape to wall.

Procedure:

1. Read, or ask a volunteer to read, Acts 4:32 aloud. **How does this verse describe the believers? What did the believers all do?** Volunteers respond.

2. Divide class into pairs. Give each pair of students index cards and a marker. Students print the words to Acts 4:32, three words on each card. Students add the Bible reference to the last card. Pairs then work together to memorize the verse.

3. Take down large sheet of paper so that Acts 4:32 is no longer displayed. Have pairs shuffle their cards. When teacher signals, pairs race to put cards back in the correct order. The first pair to

© 2000 Gospel Light. Permission to photocopy granted. *The Great Stewardship Adventure for Kids*

finish answers one of the discussion questions or tells one way to share God's gifts with others. Repeat several times. To increase the challenge, remove several cards from each set and have pairs put the remaining cards in order again.

Age-level Tip

In an effort to be liked by their peers, children this age may often act as though an activity is boring. This does not necessarily mean that they don't want to do the activity; they may simply be afraid to show their interest in case others aren't interested. Often a brief introduction is better than a longer explanation. Then move right ahead with your activity plans, laughing with them at their jokes about activities while completely involving yourself in the activity. You will most often find that they will get involved in the activity as their comfort level increases.

SERVICE FOCUS:
Snack Share

Materials: Bible with bookmark at Acts 4:32, discussion questions, juice, cups, napkins, ingredients and utensils for the recipe you choose.

Preparation: Arrange with church leaders to serve snacks at the end of the session in an area near the church entrance or some other well-traveled area. Make sure there is a table from which the students can serve the snack.

Procedure:

1. Read, or ask a volunteer to read, Acts 4:32 aloud. **When is a time someone shared with you unexpectedly? How did it feel? Today we're going to prepare food to share with other people in our church.**

2. Students wash hands. Give each student or group of students a job to do to help prepare the snack (wash table, pour juice into cups, count out napkins, carry snack to the serving table, etc.). Choose from the following snack recipes:

Banana Wafers: Using plastic knives, students cut peeled bananas into slices. Students put each slice of banana between two vanilla wafers.

Edible Animals: Provide dried fruit, miniature marshmallows and toothpicks. Each students makes two or more animals from these items.

Fruit Snack: Provide a variety of fresh fruit, several knives and cutting boards. Students wash and cut up fruit to make a fruit salad. Students spoon fruit salad into paper cups. Top with flavored yogurt, if desired.

Decorated Sugar Cookies: Bring plain sugar cookies, plastic knives, different colors of frosting and sugar sprinkles. Collect empty plastic squeeze containers such as ketchup or mustard bottles to make no-mess frosting dispensers. Students decorate cookies with frosting and sprinkles.

3. As students work, ask discussion questions. To further extend conversation, ask the following questions:

• **Why do you think sharing with others is important?**
• **What are some ways we can help others in our church learn more about God?**

- **When are some times a kid your age might not want to share with others? What could help them do the right thing?**

   4. After session has ended and as congregation leaves worship service, volunteers invite them to have a snack. (If it is not possible to share with the entire congregation, serve food to parents as they pick up children at the end of the session.)

Teaching Tips

1. Students may use plates as trays to serve the snack.

2. Giving each student a piece of wax paper to work on will make cleanup easier.

3. Provide a tall glass of warm water in which to put used knives.

Discipline Tip

Be prepared with all the materials needed for your lesson activities. Students are likely to start misbehaving if you are unprepared with materials or are confused about instructions or procedures. Before the session begins, make sure that all the snack items are ready and that there is a table set up in an area where the congregation is likely to see it.

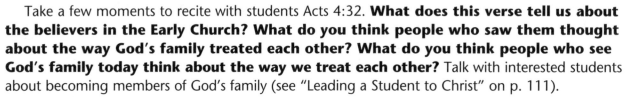

FINAL FOCUS

Stewardship Notes

Materials: Bible with bookmark at Acts 4:32, class notebook, pen.

Procedure: What are some of the things we learned today about sharing? Ask a volunteer to record students' ideas and comments in the class notebook. Volunteer then reads a few notes made during previous sessions to help students review what they have learned, reading ideas from today's session last.

   Take a few moments to recite with students Acts 4:32. **What does this verse tell us about the believers in the Early Church? What do you think people who saw them thought about the way God's family treated each other? What do you think people who see God's family today think about the way we treat each other?** Talk with interested students about becoming members of God's family (see "Leading a Student to Christ" on p. 111).

   Turning to the prayer journal section of the class notebook, volunteer writes down prayer requests and answers that students have. **Let's take a few minutes to think of a specific way we can practice stewardship by sharing the gifts God has given us with others this week.** Give students time to pray silently thanking God for the gifts He's given us and asking for God's help to find ways to share these gifts with others. Close prayer by praying for prayer requests and praising God for all the gifts He gives us and for being able to share those gifts with others.

© 2000 Gospel Light. Permission to photocopy granted. *The Great Stewardship Adventure for Kids*

KEY VERSE

"All the believers were one in heart and mind. No one claimed that any of his possessions was his own, but they shared everything they had." Acts 4:32

believers
blessing
caring
faithful
fellowship
forgiven
giving
glad
grateful
happy
helping
hopeful
humble
joyful
loving
obedient
praise
prayer
preaching
saved
sharing
singing
teaching
witnessing
worship

The Challenge ➔

Acts 2:42-47
The early Church showed love and obedience for God in lots of ways. In the puzzle below, find some words that describe the attitudes and actions of the first Christians.

```
            g n i g n i s
          b h o p e f u l
    p l u f e t a r g A s l w
    e r w o r l s n h h u m b l e i
    s p a G f a i t h f u l o d p g
    s a p i a s n e y d d o b i e n
    h y v r s H i o v a m o h t t i
    a e h e a e j e l e r s s n h h c
    r m l a d y y g n i r a c e a c
    i b g p e f e l l o w s h i p a
    n g i v i n g r w t t o k d p e
    g n w i t n e s s i n g o e y t
    w H n e v i g r o f i m a b l s
      p r e a c h i n g n i v o l o
```

___ ___ ___ ___ ___ ___ ___ ___ ___ ___ ___ ___ ___ ___ ___

___ ___ ___ ___ ___ ___ ___ ___ ___ ___ ,

___ ___ ___ ___ ___ ___ ___ ___ ___ ___ ___ ___ ___

___ ___ ___ ___ ___ ___ ___ ___ ___ ___ ___ .

© 2000 Gospel Light. Permission to photocopy granted. *The Great Stewardship Adventure for Kids*

SILLY SHARES

Cut these little cards apart.
Put all the 1s, 2s and 3s in separate piles.
Pick a card from each pile to make up a silly
(or maybe not-so-silly!) way you could share.

1 I'd let you watch	2 your favorite TV show	3 to make you happy.	1 I'd drink from	2 the same cup you use	3 even if it made me sick.	1 I'd let you borrow	2 my best coat	3 even if you failed to return it.
1 As the saying goes, "I worship	2 the ground you walk on,"	3 although I don't know what that means.	1 I'd even baby-sit	2 your dumb brother	3 to make you happy.	1 I'd let you wipe your nose on	2 my Kleenex	3 because that's the kind of person I am.
1 I'd climb	2 the highest mountain	3 to be with you.	1 I'd swim across	2 the deepest sea	3 even if I got soaked.	1 I'd stand in front of	2 a charging elephant	3 to save you.

Daily Nuggets

Share and Share Alike!

We know the members of the Early
Church were VERY good at sharing! But
how can you share? Here's some handy
advice from (where else?!) God's Word!

DAY 1

What does **Proverbs 12:25** say you can
share?

DAY 2

What items did John the Baptist mention
could be shared in **Luke 3:11**? How
could you share these things?

DAY 3

What are rich people commanded to
do with their wealth in **1 Timothy
6:17-19**? Why?

DAY 4

What three things does **Ephesians 4:32**
tell us to share with others?

DAY 5

How else can you share? For an idea,
read **Ephesians 6:18**. (Who's on your
list today?)

BONUS: If you're God's child, what
has He qualified you to share? Read
Colossians 1:12-14! WOW!

Just A Street Kid

When the 15-year-old boy asked the church volunteers for six more sandwiches to feed his brother
and sisters, they were skeptical. But he seemed so
earnest that they gave him the sand-wiches he'd
asked for. The next day, the boy, Mike, brought his
brother and sisters to the church. Something about
these caring people made Mike trust them enough
to tell his story.

Mike had been taking care of his brother and
sisters since he was nine. He'd even dropped out of
elementary school to find work to feed his brother and
sisters. Usually Mike's mom was gone; but even when
she was there, she was on drugs most of the time.
So Mike had taken on the responsibility of seeing
that his brother and sisters were clean and fed and
that they attended school. "You're going to
college!" he told them.

The members of the church wanted to help this
family! A member of the church invited Mike and
his brother and sisters to stay with them
until a home could be found. Then they
helped Mike find a good job. Mike even
joined a Christian music group. Mike
now works hard to help others as a
way of showing his thanks for the
help that was given to him.

© 2000 Gospel Light. Permission to photocopy granted. *The Great Stewardship Adventure for Kids*

For God's Glory

LIFE FOCUS

We please God when we do our best in everything.

① GETTING PREPARED

AIMS

DISCOVER why it's important to do jobs well;
RECOGNIZE that good stewards seek to please God in everything we do;
DISCUSS ways to do our various tasks to show love for God.

SCRIPTURE

Acts 16:13-15; 18:1-3

KEY VERSE

"Whatever you do, whether in word or deed, do it all
in the name of the Lord Jesus, giving thanks to God the Father through him." Colossians 3:17

Teacher's Devotional

We come to the close of our study of stewardship principles with a look at work—something that seems to occupy most of our time! Some people have "just a job"; some have a "career"; some work in their "calling" or out of their "passion" to do their work. People in New Testament times probably didn't choose their work with the freedom some of us have to choose ours, but whether we choose our work or it chooses us, the principles of how we are to work remain the same.

In ancient times, most everyone had been trained in at least one manual trade or occupation. Lydia sold expensive purple cloth and perhaps was a dyer; Aquila and Priscilla were tentmakers. Although we may think of Paul as a leader of the Sanhedrin before his conversion and a traveling evangelist and theologian afterwards, he was trained as a tentmaker as well. There was no dishonor associated with manual work; whether making tents or preaching on Mars Hill, Paul's guiding principle was unchanged. As he wrote to the believers in Colosse, "Whatever you do, whether in word or deed, do it all in the name of the Lord Jesus, giving thanks to God the Father through him" (Colossians 3:17). We are to work, doing our best at all times, thankfully and to the glory of God!

Does that seem impossible? It certainly points up our deep need for God's grace and help! As you

© 2000 Gospel Light. Permission to photocopy granted. *The Great Stewardship Adventure for Kids*

take time to reflect on your own work this week, ask the Lord to reveal to you places where you could better live up to Colossians 3:17. Think of ways God has blessed you in your work. And share freely with your students the joy of thankfully working to the glory of God!

② GETTING STARTED

Bible Blanks

Materials: Large sheet of paper, marker; optional—Bible encyclopedia.

Procedure: Draw blank lines for each letter of the word "potter." Students take turns guessing letters of the alphabet to complete the word that identifies a Bible-times job. Print correct letters on the appropriate blank lines. Print incorrect letters to the side of the blank lines. **Potters made dishes, lamps and water pots from clay. What might happen if a potter didn't do his or her best?** (The lamps and pots might leak.) Repeat with some or all of these additional words and conversation ideas. "Weaver": **A weaver's job was to weave yarn into cloth to make clothes, blankets and tents. If a weaver didn't do a good job, what might happen?** (The clothes might have holes in them. The blankets might not keep people warm.) "Scribe": **In Bible times a scribe was one of the few people who knew how to read and write. Scribes wrote important letters. Some scribes carefully copied God's Word. What are some reasons it was important for scribes always to do their best work?** "Apothecary": **An apothecary mixed and prepared medicines. People who were ill or hurt came to the apothecary for help. Apothecaries made their medicines from different parts of various plants. What could happen if apothecaries didn't do their very best work?** (Optional: Students who correctly guess the word look up information about these Bible-times jobs in a Bible encyclopedia.) **Today we're going to hear how as good stewards we can please God in everything we do.**

③ GETTING INTO GOD'S WORD

Materials: Bibles.

Bible Story

Students find Acts 16 in their Bibles. As you lead the following study, help students to discover answers in their Bibles.

What's the hardest job you have ever done? What made it difficult? What things did you learn about yourself by doing that job? Today we'll hear about some jobs people did in Bible times.

People have always worked. When God created the earth, He gave people the abilities they'd need to grow or find food, build a place to live and make clothes to keep warm. Although some people were especially good at farming or building or weaving cloth, most people still did these things for themselves. And doing their best work is one way to be good stewards and show love and thankfulness to God for all His gifts.

© 2000 Gospel Light. Permission to photocopy granted. *The Great Stewardship Adventure for Kids*

What are some ways people get food for themselves today?

Just like some families today, many Bible-times families grew their own food. Even in the city, many families had gardens. Today people might go on fishing or hunting trips for fun. But in Bible times, hunting and fishing were two major ways of getting food for the family. If there were extra food, it might be taken to the marketplace to be sold for other things that were needed.

Besides farming, fishing, hunting, building homes and making clothing, some people were carpenters who made farm tools and furniture. Some people worked with clay or metal to make pots and dishes. People who were artists or craftspeople showed their stewardship by trading with each other to get the things they needed but couldn't make. And people who could read and write had a special skill that few others had. So they often made a living doing reading and writing for people who could not write. **What kinds of things do you think scribes might read and write for others?**

In Acts 16 we meet a woman who had an interesting job. **Can you find this woman's name and her job? Look at Acts 16:14.** Lydia made and sold purple dye and purple cloth. That might not sound like a very important or interesting job to you, but this job was quite important. Because of her work, Lydia came in contact with many rich people and many members of the government.

Purple dye and the cloth made from it were very expensive and only very rich people could afford to buy it. This was because making the dye took a lot of time and work. Then it took a complicated series of steps to dye the cloth properly. Once Lydia had finished pieces of cloth to sell, she probably traveled to most of the large cities to sell her purple cloth. When Lydia heard the good news about Jesus, she became part of God's family. Once she was a member of God's family, Lydia traveled around and like a good steward, she was able to share the good news with people all over the Roman Empire. Members of God's family met together in her home. Lydia showed good stewardship because in everything she did, she worked hard and used everything she had to bring glory to God.

Paul was the man who told Lydia about Jesus. Since he'd become a follower of Jesus, Paul traveled quite a bit, telling people everywhere about Jesus. Besides telling people like Lydia about Jesus, Paul had to work to support himself. Paul had been trained in the skill of tentmaking. That means he not only made the tents, but he probably sold them as well. Because of his tentmaking skills, he met some people and a new church was started. **Who were these people and where was this church? Look at Acts 18:1-3 to find these names.** When he came to the city of Corinth, he met Priscilla and Aquila, a woman and man who were also tentmakers. They went into business together while Paul lived in that city. As Paul worked, he talked with Aquila and Priscilla. Soon they became followers of Jesus, too! And doing their best in their work was one way they could show their love for God.

Paul worked hard and used his skill at tentmaking to make money. He was able to provide for his own needs as he traveled from city to city to tell others about Jesus. Because he didn't need help from the people he visited, Paul was able to go into the poorest areas. Paul worked hard and used his job and everything he had to bring glory to God.

Today, tents are usually made in factories, out of fabrics that didn't even exist when Paul made tents. And clothes (even purple clothes) come to us already colored. Traveling to sell things, of course, is a LOT easier than it was when Paul and Lydia traveled in boats or on donkeys or simply walked from place to place.

But one thing has not changed: What God says about the WAY we work and WHY we work stays the same. He wants us to do the very best we can in whatever we do, even if it is a hard job, because it brings glory to Him! Another thing that is still the same as in Bible times is this: We can always ask God to help us do our best at everything we do. And He promises to help us if we ask Him!

© 2000 Gospel Light. Permission to photocopy granted. *The Great Stewardship Adventure for Kids*

Conclusion

Our attitudes about work can show if we are good stewards of the time and abilities God has given each of us. God wants us to do the very best we can in whatever we do, whether the jobs we have are hard or easy, whether we like them or can't stand them. Knowing it pleases God is all the reason we need to work hard, have a good attitude and do our best in EVERYTHING we do.

24 GETTING FOCUSED

Use these discussion questions as you lead students in one or more of the Getting Focused activities:

- **How are the Bible-times jobs we heard about today different from jobs your parents have? jobs you have? How are these jobs still the same?**
- **What are some of the jobs you have to do at home? at school? at church? with your friends?**
- **Do you always feel like doing your best work? Why or why not? Why would it be important to do your best at each?**
- **What job or task do you really like to do? dislike to do?**
- **Jesus promises to always be with members of His family. What are some ways He can help a kid your age do your best when you're at school? at home?** (Give courage when giving an oral report. Give patience when helping a younger brother or sister.)
- **When is a time you need Jesus' help to do your best? What are some ways you can do things differently so that you do your best work at a job you don't like to do?**

ACTIVE FOCUS:
Post-it Pandemonium

Materials: Bibles, discussion questions, index cards, marker, pencils, Post-it Notes.

Preparation: Print discussion questions on index cards with marker.

Procedure:

1. Read, or ask a volunteer to read, Colossians 3:17 aloud. **This verse tells us that no matter what job we're doing, if we do our best, we can show we love God. This doesn't mean God expects us to be PERFECT in everything we do. God understands that we sometimes make mistakes, especially when we're learning something new. But we are to always do our very best. What are some of the jobs you do every day? How would you do them if you were doing them to bring glory to God?** (Do my best work. Work hard. Follow God's commands. Be thankful for the job and the ability to do the job.)

2. Students number off. Give each student a Post-it Note and a pencil. Each student writes his or her number on a Post-it Note. Students then randomly place notes around the room in unusual but visible places.

3. Students walk randomly around the room. After a few moments say, "Stop." Each student quickly finds and places a hand on a Post-it Note. (Only one person may touch each note.) Call out a number. Student touching note with that number receives an index card from you and reads aloud

© 2000 Gospel Light. Permission to photocopy granted. *The Great Stewardship Adventure for Kids*

the question. Call out a second number. Student with hand on second number answers the question or asks a volunteer to answer. (Optional: Instead of asking volunteer to answer question, student calls out "Up!" or "Down!" and the student with the next number up or down answers the question.) Continue with other cards, repeating if necessary, as time permits.

Teaching Tip

This game works well with small or large groups. However, in larger groups, you may wish to call out more than one number for each round and have several students answer each question.

Discipline Tips

1. If students are giving quick answers simply to get on with the game, set a 10-second time limit for thinking. Students may not give an answer before the time limit is up.

2. If your room is too small or if students are too active, students sit to play the game by passing the Post-it Notes (or numbered index cards).

Alternate Activities

1. Have students think up various tasks that kids would do and write one on each Post-it Note. Collect notes, place them at random on the walls around the room, and divide group into pairs or trios. Send each group to an area where a Post-it Note is on the wall. Pairs or trios role-play the task on the Post-it Note to the best of their ability. Use the discussion questions to expand conversation about each task.

2. In addition to, or instead of, printing discussion questions on index cards, print the Life Focus for each of the lessons in this course. The first student whose number you call will read the Life Focus from an index card. The second student whose number you call will give an example of good stewardship that fits that Life Focus.

ART FOCUS:
Scribes and Scrolls

Materials: Bibles, brown grocery bags, markers, yarn or jute, scissors.
Procedure:

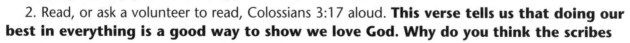

1. **Why do you think it's important to know how to read and write? What are some things you couldn't do if you didn't know how to read or write?** Volunteers respond. **In Bible times, only a few people knew how to read and write. What were these people called?** (Scribes.) **The word "scribe" in Hebrew means "one who writes." Some scribes carefully copied God's Word. That's because there were no printing presses or copy machines in Bible times.**

2. Read, or ask a volunteer to read, Colossians 3:17 aloud. **This verse tells us that doing our best in everything is a good way to show we love God. Why do you think the scribes**

who copied God's Word had to be careful and do their best work? (If they made a mistake, people wouldn't know what God's Word really said.) **What are some jobs you have? Why would it be important to do your best at your jobs?** Volunteers respond. Use discussion questions to continue conversation as students follow instructions below to create scrolls.

3. Students cut grocery bags to make a rectangular sheet of paper and then crumple paper into a tight ball. After smoothing paper out, students repeat crumpling process several times to soften paper and give it an ancient look. Students copy the words of Colossians 3:17 onto papers and then roll papers up like scrolls. Using scissors, students cut a length of yarn or jute to tie scrolls closed.

Teaching Tips

1. **What do we make paper from today?** (Trees.) Explain how paper was made in Bible Times. **In Bible times, paper was made from the stems of a plant called papyrus. Papyrus strips were beaten together into long sheets and rolled to make scrolls.**

2. Understanding life in Bible times will help students bridge the gap between their lives and the lives of Bible people. Becoming familiar with the ways Bible people lived will help students recognize that people the Bible tells about are not fantasy characters.

Enrichment Idea

Students use paintbrushes and black tempera paint to paint the words of Colossians 3:17 onto scrolls.

Alternate Activity

Provide air-drying clay, several rolling pins, table knives and pencils. Give each student a fist-sized ball of clay. Students flatten balls of clay with their hands and use a rolling pin to form a rectangular slab about 1/2-inch (1.25-cm) thick. Students use pencils to etch letters in the clay. Let dry.

- -

FINAL FOCUS

Stewardship Notes

Materials: Bible with bookmark at Colossians 3:17, class notebook, pen; optional—materials for a mural (large paper, markers, masking tape).

Procedure: What different Bible-time jobs did we talk about today? (Potter, weaver, scribe, apothecary, tentmaker, seller of purple.) **What are some of the other things we learned about jobs today?** Ask a volunteer to record students' responses in the class notebook. After students have given answers, volunteer reads aloud from the class notebook a few points from the previous lessons to help students remember what they have learned.

Read Colossians 3:17 aloud. **In whose name are we supposed to be working? Why is doing our very best in everything we do an important part of stewardship?**

(Optional: After discussion, show mural materials. Students write or draw something on mural about what they learned and add their name or initials to what is written. After session has ended, ask volunteers to help you place mural in a hallway, vestibule or other public area.)

Take a few minutes to review the prayer journal with students to see what prayers God has answered during this course. Invite each student to pray a sentence prayer, thanking God for whatever he or she learned that has most helped him or her. Close by thanking God for His gifts and asking for His help to do our best in everything we do.

© 2000 Gospel Light. Permission to photocopy granted. *The Great Stewardship Adventure for Kids*

THE LIVING IT! PAGE

SESSION 13

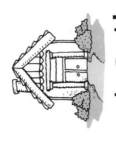

Family Builder

Do a newspaper search with your family. Find out where there are needs and opportunities for service in your neighborhood. How could your family serve?

Need some help thinking up stuff you could do to serve the Lord by serving others?

TRY THIS

Stewardship Chart-O-Matic!

Instructions: To find some good ideas, and a lot of not-so-good ideas, fill in the appropriate numbered blanks with words or phrases from the numbered columns. For example, if you took the first word in each list, the sentence would say, "I could serve my Lord by praying for others and by contributing my time, talent and even some of my treasure (my allowance), because I love the Lord." There are tons of combinations—most of which are worthless!

I could serve (1) _____ by (2) _____

and by (3) _____, because (4) _____

1	**2**
my Lord	praying for others
my friends	singing in Bible study
myself	preaching in Bible study
if I had a serveboard . . . or is it "surfboard"?	keeping my mouth shut in Bible study
dinner	taking a much-needed bath
in the army	using a tennis racket
tennis balls	gum

3	**4**
contributing my time, talent and even some of my treasure (my allowance)	I love the Lord.
	that's what stewardship's all about.
bringing my best friend to visit my youth group	I'm sitting here with nothing else to do.
bringing my youth group to visit my best friend	they're holding me hostage.
ignoring this game	I'm just a naturally wonderful person.
calling the police	I blacked out.
the way	why?
two o'clock	

Topic for Conversation with God

Dear God, please show me ways to serve You!

© 2000 Gospel Light. Permission to photocopy granted. *The Great Stewardship Adventure for Kids*

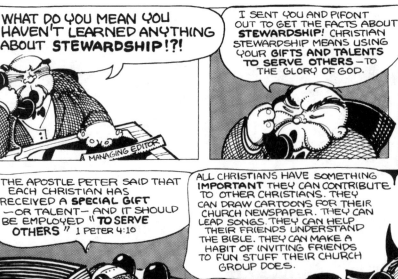

Stewardship is a term derived from the role of stewards in biblical times. The steward was in charge of and took care of the household or estate belonging to his master. Christians need to recognize that we are stewards, not owners, of everything God gives us.

KEY VERSE

"Whatever you do, whether in word or deed, do it all in the name of the Lord Jesus, giving thanks to God the Father through him." Colossians 3:17

Daily Nuggets

Every Wakin' Minute

So just how do we do everything in the name of the Lord and please Him in everything we do? Read some hot hints from God's Word.

DAY 1
Psalm 34:1-4
How often does David say he will praise God? (Do you suppose *he* talked to God every wakin' minute?) When can you praise God?

DAY 2
Psalm 62:8
God's people are supposed to trust Him and pour out their hearts (pray!) to Him—how often? (every wakin' minute?) When do you need to trust God and talk to Him?

DAY 3
Ephesians 6:18
Pray in the Spirit on *what* occasions? (like, every wakin' minute?) Write a prayer request list for today.

DAY 4
Philippians 4:4-7
Rejoice in the Lord *how often?* Talk to God about *what?* (instead of *worrying* every wakin' minute?) Thank God for listening to your prayers.

DAY 5
2 Corinthians 9:8
God is able to make *what* abound? at what time? Sounds like He gives pretty complete help! (every wakin' minute!) What good thing can God help you do today?

© 2000 Gospel Light. Permission to photocopy granted. *The Great Stewardship Adventure for Kids*

Leading a Student to Christ

Many adult Christians look back to their upper elementary years as the time when they accepted Christ as Savior. Not only are fourth-, fifth- and sixth-graders able to understand the difference between right and wrong and their own personal need of forgiveness, they are interested in Jesus' death and resurrection as the means by which God provides salvation. In addition, students at this age are capable of growing in their faith through prayer, Bible reading, worship and service.

However, students this age are still limited in their understanding, and immature in following through on their intentions and commitments. As such, they need thoughtful, patient guidance in coming to know Christ personally and continuing to grow in Him.

1. Pray.

Ask God to prepare the students in your class to receive the good news about Jesus and prepare you to effectively communicate with them.

2. Present the good news.

Use words and phrases that students understand. Avoid symbolism that will confuse these literal-minded thinkers. Discuss these points slowly enough to allow time for thinking and comprehending.

a. "God wants you to become His child. Do you know why God wants you in His family?" (See 1 John 4:8.)

b. "You and all the people in the world have done wrong things. The Bible word for doing wrong is "sin." What do you think should happen to us when we sin?" (See Romans 6:23.)

c. "God loves you so much, He sent His Son to die on the cross for your sin. Because Jesus never sinned, He is the only one who can take the punishment for your sin." (See 1 Corinthians 15:3; 1 John 4:14.)

d. "Are you sorry for your sin? Tell God that you are. Do you believe Jesus died to take the punishment for your sin? If you tell God you are sorry for your sin and tell Him you do believe and accept Jesus' death to take away your sin, God forgives all your sin." (See John 1:12.)

e. "The Bible says that when you believe in Jesus, God's Son, you receive God's gift of eternal life. This gift makes you a child of God. (See John 3:16.) This means God is with you now and forever."

Give students many opportunities to think about what it means to be a Christian; expose them to a variety of lessons and descriptions of the meaning of salvation to aid their understanding.

3. Talk personally with the student.

Talking about salvation one-on-one creates the opportunity to ask and answer questions. Ask questions that move the student beyond simple yes or no answers or recitation of memorized information. Ask what-do-you-think kinds of questions such as

"Why do you think it's important to . . . ?"

"What are some things you really like about Jesus?"

"Why do you think that Jesus had to die because of wrong things you and I have done?"

"What difference do you think it makes for a person to be forgiven?"

Answers to these open-ended questions will help you discern how much the student does or does not understand.

4. Offer opportunities without pressure.

Fourth-, fifth- and sixth-graders are still children, vulnerable to being manipulated by adults. A good way to guard against coercing a student's response is to simply pause periodically and ask, "Would you like to hear more about this now or at another time?" Loving acceptance of the student, even when he or she is not fully interested in pursuing the matter, is crucial in building and maintaining positive attitudes toward becoming part of God's family.

5. Give time to think and pray.

There is great value in encouraging a student to think and pray about what you have said before making a response. Also allow moments for quiet thinking about questions you ask.

6. Respect the student's response.

Whether or not a student declares faith in Jesus Christ, there is a need for adults to accept the student's action. There is also a need to realize that a student's initial responses to Jesus are just the beginning of a lifelong process of growing in the faith.

7. Guide the student in further growth.

Here are three important parts in the nurturing process.

a. Talk regularly about your relationship with God. As you talk about your relationship, the student will begin to feel that it's OK to talk about such things. Then you can comfortably ask the student to share his or her thoughts and feelings, and encourage the student to ask questions of you.

b. Prepare the student to deal with doubts. Emphasize that certainty about salvation is not dependent on our feelings or doing enough good deeds. Show the student places in God's Word that clearly declare that salvation comes by grace through faith (John 1:12; Ephesians 2:8,9; Hebrews 11:6; 1 John 5:11).

c. Teach the student to confess all sin. This means agreeing with God that we really have sinned. Assure the student that confession always results in forgiveness.

© 2000 Gospel Light. Permission to photocopy granted. *The Great Stewardship Adventure for Kids*

Glossary

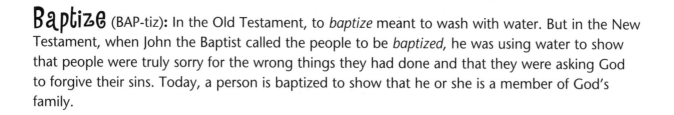

Atonement (uh-TOHN-mehnt): To make up for a wrong act; to become friends again. In the Bible, *atonement* usually means to become friends with God after sin has separated us from Him. In the Old Testament, the Israelites brought sacrifices to *atone* for their sins. The New Testament teaches that Jesus Christ made *atonement* for our sins when He died on the cross. Because Jesus died to "make up" for our sins, we can have peace with God.

Baptize (BAP-tiz): In the Old Testament, to *baptize* meant to wash with water. But in the New Testament, when John the Baptist called the people to be *baptized*, he was using water to show that people were truly sorry for the wrong things they had done and that they were asking God to forgive their sins. Today, a person is baptized to show that he or she is a member of God's family.

Believe (bee-LEEV): To have faith or to trust that something is true. The Bible tells us that we can *believe* that Jesus Christ is God's Son and trust Him to keep His promise to forgive sins. We show that we *believe* that God loves us and wants what is best for us by obeying His commands.

Condemn (kuhn-DEHM): 1. To find someone guilty of doing something wrong and to declare or pronounce a punishment. 2. To be against or disapprove of something because it is wrong.

Confess (kuhn-FEHS): To *confess* means to tell or agree about what is true. *Confess* sometimes means telling God your sins. *Confess* can also mean to say in front of other people that you believe that Jesus is God's Son and that He died and rose again to forgive you of your sins.

Conscience (KON-shuhns): A feeling about what is right and what is wrong; a sense of knowing what is good and what is bad.

Faith (FAYTH): *Faith* has two meanings in the Bible. 1. To be certain about the things we cannot see or to trust someone because of who he or she is. For example, a Christian has faith that Jesus is God's Son. 2. "The faith" means the whole message about Jesus Christ—that He is God's Son and that He came to take the punishment for our sin so that we may become members of God's family.

© 2000 Gospel Light. Permission to photocopy granted. *The Great Stewardship Adventure for Kids*

Faithful (FAYTH-fuhl): Always loyal and trustworthy. God is *faithful*. We can always trust Him to do whatever He has promised. We are also to be *faithful* in doing what is right.

Forgive (for-GIHV): To stop feeling angry and to stop blaming a person for something wrong he or she has done; to be friends again. God *forgives* everyone who believes that Jesus died to take the punishment for his or her sins. When God *forgives* a person, God forgets the person's sins forever. God instructs Christians to *forgive* each other in The same way He has *forgiven* them.

Holy Spirit (HOH-lee SPIH-riht): the personal but unseen power and presence of God in the world. The book of Acts tells us that the *Holy Spirit* came to followers of Jesus in a special way after Jesus had gone back to heaven. The *Holy Spirit* lives within all people who have had their sins forgiven. Jesus said the *Holy Spirit* is our helper and comforter. The *Holy Spirit* teaches us truth about God. He helps us understand the Bible and helps us pray in the right way. He gives us the power and strength to do what Jesus wants.

Justification (juhs-tih-fih-KAY-shuhn): God's action of treating sinners who have faith in Jesus Christ as if they had never sinned. God forgives their sin and becomes their friend. God also gives them the power to live right. *Justification* is possible because Jesus Christ died to take the punishment for sin.

Manage (MAN-ihj): To be in control or in charge of; to use wisely and care for. God gives us many gifts to *manage*. By using things well, taking good care of them and not being wasteful, we are *managing* God's gifts.

Reconcile (REHCK-uhn-sil): To help people who have been enemies become friends. In the New Testament, the word usually refers to bringing God and people together again through Jesus' life, death and resurrection. Sin separates people from God, but by dying, Jesus took the punishment for sin. When a person comes to know and love Jesus, he or she learns to love God instead of being His enemy. When this happens, the person is *reconciled* to God.

Redeem (ree-DEEM): To buy back. In Bible times, a person could pay a slave's owner whatever the slave was worth and then set the slave free. The slave had been *redeemed* by the person who had bought the slave and then set him or her free. The New Testament tells us that by dying, Jesus paid the price to "buy us back" and set us free from our slavery to sin.

Repent (ree-PEHNT): *Repent* means to turn around and go in the opposite direction. In the Bible, to *repent* means that you stop doing wrong actions and start doing what God says is right. *Repentance* always involves making a change away from sin and towards God.

© 2000 Gospel Light. Permission to photocopy granted. *The Great Stewardship Adventure for Kids*

Righteous (RI-chuhs): Thinking and doing what is right and holy. The word is used in three ways in the Bible: 1. To tell what God is like; He does only what is right and holy. 2. A person who has accepted Jesus as Savior is looked at by God as being free from the guilt of sin. God sees the person as being *righteous*. 3. People who are members of God's family show their love for Him by living in *righteous* ways. They do what is right and holy.

Steward (STOO-uhrd): Someone who takes care of something for its real owner. In Bible times, a *steward* was in charge of another man's household. The *steward* directed the other servants, made sure meals were served and made sure all the expenses were paid. In New Testament times, Jesus' followers were instructed to act as *stewards* of all God's gifts. This involved using time, talents, possessions and themselves in God's work.

Stewardship (STOO-uhrd-shihp): The careful and responsible management of something belonging to someone else. As members of God's family, all that we have belongs to God, so we are to be careful and wise in the way we use all of God's gifts. These gifts include the earth and all its resources, the possessions and money God gives us, our time, our talents and each other.

Talent (TAL-ehnt): In New-Testament times, a large amount of silver or gold worth a huge amount of money. One *talent* was considered to be the amount of money a working man would earn in about ten years. Today, talents are abilities God has given us.

Tithe (TITH): To give God one-tenth of what you earn. For example, if you had ten dimes, you would *tithe* by giving one dime back to God.

Trust (TRUHST): To have faith in, or believe in the honesty and worth of someone. As members of God's family, we can trust in Him with all our heart, mind and spirit. *Trust* also means a firm reliance, faith or confident belief in something. Finally, *trust* can mean something given to be cared for in the interest of someone else. For example, the earth God created has been given to us as a trust for us to care for and manage.

Trustworthy (TRUHST-wuhr-thee): To deserve or be worthy of someone's faith or confidence. God is *trustworthy* because we can always depend on Him to keep His promises. Because God has given us so many gifts, we are to be *trustworthy* stewards—taking care of God's gifts carefully and dependably.

© 2000 Gospel Light. Permission to photocopy granted. *The Great Stewardship Adventure for Kids*